THE BUSINESS GROWTH ENGINE SECRETS FOR ENTREPRENEURS

POPUP
YOUR
E-COMMERCE

POPUP
YOUR
E-COMMERCE
BUSINESS

THE STEP-BY-STEP SECRET GUIDE TO SUCCESS

How to **Connect with Customers** In Person & **Grow Online Traffic** and **Sales** to your E-Commerce Business Using Pop-Up Shop as the **GROWTH ENGINE**

THE BUSINESS GROWTH ENGINE SECRETS

BY
DAMIAN POWELL

The Pop-up Shop Business Tetralogy Series

Make Pop-up Shop the Growth Engine for your E-commerce business to reap exponential financial rewards. For more information, email: damian@popupshopbusiness.com.

Paperback ISBN: 978-1-7379373-8-8
Hardcover ISBN: 978-1-7379373-5-7
e-Book ISBN: 978-1-7379373-6-4
Audiobook ISBN: 978-1-7379373-7-1

This Book Is Dedicated To

The small business owners in Hampton Roads, Virginia, and globally:

I extend my heartfelt gratitude for the incredible support I received from countless entrepreneurs worldwide during my previous book project. Your encouragement has truly been a blessing and a profound inspiration for me to present this publication to you. With an unwavering dedication to the Pop-up Shop Business Initiative, I am consistently filled with enthusiasm to assist entrepreneurs in attaining their personal and professional aspirations through my mission.

May this book serve as a valuable resource, bridging the knowledge gap that is crucial for your company's success. If it proves instrumental in fulfilling your desires, I take immense pride in declaring that this initiative continues to thrive.

CONTENTS

INTRODUCTION

Popup Your E-commerce Business

As our lives evolve, so too does the online sphere, offering entrepreneurs endless opportunities to thrive. Navigating the vast and ever-changing landscape of technology requires keeping communication channels open. With this in mind, allow me to introduce you to the pop-up shop framework, a modern strategy designed to propel your e-commerce business to new heights.

Since the publication of "*Popup Your Startup*," many brands have embraced this approach, unleashing creative concepts, debuting unique products, and engaging in community events. Pop-ups flourish on innovative ideas and compelling presentations that capture the imagination of the world.

Pop-up shops play a vital role in increasing sales and improving brand visibility, benefiting individuals with side hustles, startup entrepreneurs, traditional brick-and-mortar stores, and online businesses, all while working with limited resources. These principles, known as "The Launchpad Principles" and outlined in

"Popup Your Startup," serve as the basis of this book. The operational framework of pop-up shops is designed to boost your e-commerce launchpad, which refers to how your company was initially launched and the subsequent use of pop-ups to support its growth. If your business primarily operates as a pop-up shop, the other three launchpad strategies serve as accelerators.

In addition to their magical appeal, pop-up shops offer lower risk exposure and require significantly less capital than permanent physical storefronts and online businesses. They are short-term responsibilities with minimal expenses. The secrets revealed in this book will position you to seize a lifetime of opportunities and thrive in the e-commerce sector.

Pop-ups can be open for as little as a day or extend up to six months or even a year. Since they are temporary, these shops don't demand the usual overhead costs associated with permanent physical buildings, such as long-term rent, protection agreements, physical accommodations, or staffing in some cases. Instead, all you need is something to sell or promote and a venue to do so. With that, pop-ups will surely bring confidence and flexibility to your online operation.

After all, the transfer of physical to digital happens naturally, with most human interactions occurring in today's information age. There are no limits to the online business opportunities that lie ahead by using this approach.

Everyone ultimately functions in the digital world at a moment's notice, and it is merely obvious to us. Those intimidated by technology and refusing to buy, sell, or communicate across the web will soon realize that adaptation to at least one is necessary and inevitable. We operate our daily life routines accompanied by the many ones and zeros that connect us personally and transaction-ally.

Many of our tasks done from dusk until dawn are re-layed via the World Wide Web through any medium of choice. Whether it is our phones, computers, tablets, watches, or any other smart devices, the alphanumeric connectiveness is endless, and communication is simpler and easier than ever be-fore. With these existing digital influences that define how we in-terconnect as people, having a pop-up shop operation is what's needed to support your e-commerce.

A face-to-face experience is where wave signals of technology begin to link us as humans beyond the physical gamut. This oc-curs as people interact in person, and then suddenly, that inter-action is transferred over to the digital world. This happens, for example, due to a possible courtship between prospective part-ners, a new or developing friendship, an initial business partner-ship, or a business-to-client relationship. These associations may start with a physical encounter before meeting again over cyber-space (internet). The initial physical contact typically graduates into friendship or a follow-on social media engagement, zoom meeting, or a scheduled future physical dealing. All of this re-minds us of how powerful and impactful digital web is, and it's advantageous for you to reap the benefits.

Now, you must be wondering how this will build and grow my e-commerce business. It will not only grow your online presence but astronomically increase traffic, sales, and longevity. Study this guide, and your business will become bulletproof to failure. You are essentially taking your online business offline, then back online, and repeating the effort using people and technology. It gets easier and better over time as you act decisively and imple-ment the strategies that I have outlined.

Understanding the value and utilizing this framework for overall growth is the dream of many entrepreneurs. In this book, I will guide you through ten secret strategies that will empower you to *"Popup Your E-commerce"* business. The transformation from physical interactions at pop-up shop venues to the online web will be explained comprehensively, going beyond the mere presence of a website, social media, or online marketplaces. This business development initiative will dispel the notion that having a great product or service is enough for customers to magically find and connect with you online.

You are closer than ever to the results you have always hoped for your e-commerce website and overall enterprise. After all, maybe most of what you have tried before just simply did not work as you expected.

Continue reading and I will show you how to use a pop-up shop operation as a business and marketing tool for operational efficiency to create financial gains. After reading these secret guidelines, you will:

> ➢ Fully understand how to drive website traffic through your funnels and use proper SEO strategies.

> ➢ Deliver an aligned purposeful brand message online and offline simultaneously.

> ➢ Learn how to build rapport and customer engagement online and offline.

> ➢ Know how to track and streamline your efforts and stay committed to the journey.

Moreover, you will garner comprehensive knowledge of generating direct, organic, paid, and social media traffic. Knowing these secret arsenals for your e-commerce business is a sure way to build a competitive advantage.

Only those entrepreneurs who think creatively, outside the box, and persistently without hesitation or indecisiveness emerge victorious. If this resonates with you, reading this book cover to cover will guarantee the results you have always desired.

Moreover, bringing your revolutionary idea to the world, one that can make a positive impact and improve lives, is never easy. However, it's worth pursuing if there is a market need. If you haven't read my previous book on pop-up shops, I encourage you to do so. It will help you analyze the merits of your products or services, considering factors such as market need, size, and your market segment.

This publication will guide you on how to meet some of your clients in person and invite them to your social and e-commerce places, ensuring you don't solely rely on aimlessly attracting customers to your online business. By incorporating pop-up shops into your online presence, along with brick-and-mortar stores, e-commerce websites, and online marketplaces, you will expand your digital footprint, generate more leads, and increase customer acquisition, brand awareness, and revenue.

Another question you might be wondering about is whether this book is right for you. Allow me to clarify.

Who would benefit from reading this book?

If you are currently pursuing entrepreneurship or considering it, and you operate any of the following types of businesses listed below, then I recommend that you continue reading. However, let's first recap the basic definition of e-commerce or conducting business online.

E-commerce refers to the electronic buying or selling of products over the internet. It is commonly known as online business and typically involves operating solely through the internet without a physical location for selling products or services. For the framework of the pop-up shop business initiative, an e-commerce business can also include a traditional physical storefront that sells products online, known as "online retail." Additionally, a purely online e-commerce website is referred to as a pure e-commerce business that you should make note of. Furthermore, another term, "online marketplace," such as eBay, is a platform where products are displayed and sold. If you operate any of the business types mentioned, reading this book could make a significant difference between success and failure. The choice is yours!

Physical Storefront Online Retail

This refers to having a physical brick-and-mortar store while also offering products for sale online. It means engaging in online retailing. Brick-and-mortar signifies the physical presence of a business in a building or structure. A brick-and-mortar business is a company that owns or leases retail shops, production facilities, or warehouses for its operations. As the owner, you are responsible for employing the necessary resources and tools to sell your goods and services online. An example of an online retailer is Walmart Supercenter, where you can purchase household goods online or visit their physical store. Nowadays, most traditional businesses have some portion of their revenue coming from online retail sales and pop-up shops. "*Popup Your Storefront*" at www.popupyourstorefront.com provides insights on how to accomplish this.

Pure E-commerce Business

Pure e-commerce refers to conducting business exclusively via the internet. It involves operating a website where you sell products or services without owning a physical location for customers to visit, such as brick-and-mortar stores and pop-up shops. If I may add, initially, my startup business was purely e-commerce until I realized the value of having a pop-up shop. The commonly used term for this type of online business has been an e-commerce storefront, which is now often referred to as an e-commerce business.

Online Marketplace Business

In addition to online retail and pure e-commerce, there are other online shopping websites available, such as Etsy, Amazon, Bonanza, and eBay. These places offer e-commerce opportunities and are known as online storefront marketplaces. Having these digital marketplaces along with your e-commerce website and physical storefront online retail can provide an additional revenue stream. Many startup entrepreneurs utilize this type of online business before establishing an e-commerce website or brick-and-mortar store. If you are one such individual, I recommend using pop-up shops to assist with your growth efforts. Including these marketplaces in your online presence will generate more leads, increase customer acquisition, enhance brand awareness, and boost sales.

Therefore, expanding your e-commerce storefront or online business range into the pop-up shop process will guarantee overarching positive long-term results for your company. Your dream clients will appreciate the accessibility of your service and merchandise coming from two or more channels.

Begin the Pop-up Shop Journey

Customers are constantly connected through their devices, whether in stores or at pop-up shops. As a popupreneur, your responsibility is to guide and instruct them to connect with you online—your website, social media, and more. This simple yet powerful approach fosters connectivity and engagement.

The world is immersed in cyberspace, and by inviting your customers to visit your business online, you tap into the wealth of opportunities it presents. The World Wide Web serves as an information system designed to fulfill human experiences. Seizing the digital stratosphere and making pop-up shops the growth engine for your online business is a game-changing move. This framework will empower you to build a strong foundation, accelerate growth, and achieve instant profit.

Are you ready to unlock the potential of pop-up shops and revolutionize your e-commerce business? Let's embark on this journey together.

SECRET GUIDE #1
Understanding the Power of Pop-ups

A New Opportunity for Sustained E-commerce Growth.

I f you're familiar with the launch efforts of my company, isls-nac, also known as Taste Vacation, you probably know that my e-commerce website didn't fare well initially. It was quite evident that my hopes and dreams of conquering the world with my novel idea were much further from reality than I had initially thought. I was under the false assumption that my e-commerce website would instantly get traffic and generate sales upon its launch. It was devastating to realize that it wasn't as easy as I had imagined. Many other e-commerce business owners seemed to boast about their online success, but they often neglected to mention the crucial details that budding entrepreneurs like me were unaware of. In this book, I will share these vital specifics with you, equipping you with the knowledge necessary for the growth of your online business.

Despite the slow start, I maintained my optimism about the opportunities offered by operating online. As a result, I committed myself to working 12-18 hours a day to acquire the knowledge I needed. Now, I have the privilege of sharing the lessons I've learned with you.

Although my business faced setbacks, I managed to stay afloat, remain relevant, and continue to overcome the challenges. During my self-study and research, I discovered a new opportunity: "*The Pop-up Shop Business.*" This new opportunity can be executed in four ways, depending on your entrepreneurship pursuits, and "*Popup Your E-commerce*" is one of them.

By combining pop-up shop techniques with my acquired knowledge of Digital Marketing and Search Engine Optimization (SEO), I confidently continued to build my e-commerce store and establish islsnac's online authority.

This newfound opportunity eventually led to the publication of "*Popup Your Startup*" and this book, both part of my Tetralogy series. Pure e-commerce stores and other online selling methods have their own set of challenges. Understanding the power of pop-ups in boosting e-commerce is a true blessing for myself and many others who have implemented this business concept, yielding proven and successful results.

Furthermore, my journey of running pop-up shops has provided insights into the world of various other online businesses. Through numerous interviews and research conducted among entrepreneurs, I discovered a truth that I had always suspected. Contrary to what many so-called online coaches, agencies, and gurus claim on social media, running an e-commerce site is not as effortless as they make it seem. Their advertisements and posts can be misleading, failing to convey the months or even years of work required to achieve significant online earnings.

Moreover, there are specific criteria that must be met before your potential customers will part with their money. You need to provide a solution to their problem and clearly illustrate the purpose of your product or service. Only then will they be inclined to accept what you offer. There's no such thing as getting rich quick; building an online business or any venture takes time. Now is the time to seize the moment and utilize pop-up shops to accelerate growth.

It's interesting to note that when you ask online shop owners about their site performance, their answers are often the same: "I'm doing great!" However, this is often not the case. Through studying and understanding the intricacies of building an online business, it becomes clear that many e-commerce websites face challenges. Unfortunately, entrepreneurs often fail to acknowledge and address the deficiencies that lead to underperformance. In some cases, they lack the core knowledge required to launch a competitive website, and that's where this book becomes an asset.

During my journey, I relied on a few helpful analytics tools to build and optimize my own business, as well as those of my dedicated clients. These tools are designed to assess and understand competitors' authority level, performance, and customer behavior. Ahrefs and SEMrush are two of my favorite tools, both of which offer free or paid services. Whenever an entrepreneur boasts about their online success, I simply input their URL into one of these tools. The results are often the same: lack of authority, low traffic volume, minimal sales, and inadequate optimization. I frequently recommend using pop-ups to leverage the online building process. This is one of the reasons why I advocate for the power of pop-up shops since it has proven effective for my business, both online and offline, and it can do the same for you.

The results obtained through the pop-up shop business opportunity have brought extraordinary gains to my own startup and seasoned physical storefront companies that employ my initiative. It's my duty to share these secrets, which are not really secrets at all. Many of the individuals I've had the privilege to mentor have achieved encouraging results for their enterprises. I urge you to keep an open mind and embrace this transformative breakthrough. I believe that incorporating pop-ups into your company's operations is one of the keys to business growth and success.

If you're starting to doubt whether this approach will work for you, what comes next will reveal how pop-ups can make your company thrive. However, it's important to acknowledge that mishaps are bound to happen as you embark on this journey of building your business. Mistakes will be made, and unexpected events will occur, whether due to your own blunders or external circumstances. I advise you to be aware and anticipate any pitfalls by creating well-planned contingencies. In Secret Guide #7 of "*Popup Your Startup*," you'll find a step-by-step guide on developing a contingency plan. Visit www.popupyourstartup.com.

Additionally, seek out relevant books, invest in professional self-development guides like online courses and training, and remain committed to the grind, regardless of the challenges you may face.

Understandably, you might be wondering how you'll survive with these demanding tasks. No need to worry, as I've included one of my favorite secrets for overcoming adversity in this very book. In Secret Guide #10, "Stay Committed to the Grind," you'll find valuable advice on persevering through difficulties.

I'm not trying to be pessimistic or discourage your efforts, but if you believe that the world will discover you or that virality will strike within minutes, then perhaps it's best to stop reading. Nothing you do moving forward, or any results you achieve, will be based on luck. The guidance provided in this book, as well as in any of my pop-up shop book series, is deliberately aimed at yielding positive and desired results. It's important to note that achieving positive results doesn't mean you won't encounter challenges.

This brings me to a few important topics worth sharing. Throughout my journey as an e-commerce startup owner, I've identified four things that I consider key indicators, which are explained in this section. These indicators shed light on why pop-ups are of great importance. I encourage you to study them as they can be helpful in both the best and worst of times.

You will discover how your online business can maximize entrepreneurial efforts by applying the pop-up shop opportunities. Read on to learn how you can utilize pop-ups to gain a competitive advantage and stay relevant.

Outlined below are the key indicators and benefits that successful popupreneurs have used to propel their businesses forward. By understanding and implementing these principles, you can harness the power of pop-up stores as the growth engine for both present and future online successes. These indicators are ever-present concepts that, when properly identified and implemented, add value to your business, foster unexpected insights, and nurture creativity as you actively incorporate pop-ups into your e-commerce strategy.

Key Indicators and Benefits (KIB)

Operating pop-up shops lures customers to your products and services in a cost-effective manner while also generating excitement around your brand. These temporary setups offer more than just cost savings; they play an important role in the growth of your business. With these strategies, you can ignite enthusiasm, pique customer curiosity, and boost your overall revenue. Here's a summary highlighting key indicators and advantages of operating these shops.

KIB Summarized

Drive Brand and Product Exposure – Pop-up shops enable you to showcase your brand and products in a tangible and immersive way, effectively capturing the attention of potential customers.

Test New Markets – These shops provide a low-risk opportunity to discover new markets, allowing you to gauge customer interest and demand before fully committing to expansion.

Gain Real-World Insights – By studying how customers behave and what they like in a real-world setting, you can learn more about them and use that information to continuously improve your e-commerce strategies.

Pivoting – As one of the key indicators and benefits, pivoting allows e-commerce adaptation and exploration of these new opportunities by using pop-up operations as a flexible platform for testing and refining products, services, and business plans.

As an e-commerce owner, you undoubtedly seek to give your business a competitive edge. The application of the information provided here offers an enjoyable and practical approach to promoting your brand, connecting with customers personally, and then maximizing those efforts online.

To enhance your online store, study the following four key indicators and benefits of using pop-up shop as your business growth engine:

- ➢ Drive Brand and Product Exposure
- ➢ Gain Real-World Insights
- ➢ Test New Markets
- ➢ Pivoting

By practicing these indicators, you can make your business better and take it to new heights of success online.

Drive Brand and Product Exposure

Pop-ups are established as moveable temporary physical shops that are used to offer customers immersive experiences. The primary objective is to promote your company and gain exposure. The benefits of incorporating pop-ups into an e-commerce business should not be underestimated. By showcasing your brand message and theme, your products and services can potentially become the highlight of the experience.

Product Rollout

According to a study, one of the main reasons consumers appreciate pop-up events is to stay informed about new trends. Temporary product releases or brand ideas generate excitement when introduced to the market through these shops. For example, if your e-commerce business sells seasonally associated products like unique holiday gifts, a pop-up shop can be used to pre-launch these items and gauge people's response before officially adding them to your online collection. Also, in certain cases, you can relaunch older products that may not have gained enough digital traction.

This business model shows promise and is gaining popularity everywhere, particularly during peak seasons. Whether it's holiday bazaars, Easter fairs, or summer flings, pop-ups offer year-round celebrations that bring shoppers and proprietors together. A diverse group of merchants throughout neighborhoods contributes to the abundance of selections available during these events. Pop-up entrepreneurs are not merely selling for minimal profits; they are making an impact in their respective communities. This includes retail storefront businesses showcasing new collections and startup vendors launching their businesses. And, as an e-commerce owner, you can select new or existing items from your online product page and present them directly to people.

Several unique style offerings are ideal for seasonal events, such as handmade crafts displayed at festivals, Christmas tree lots at markets, accessories/jewelry kiosks in malls, self-care products at the painted tree, and booths selling wine or mocktails with cheese.

Placing your online merchandise on pop-up shelves engages people's senses and captures the attention of passersby, which is particularly advantageous with new product rollouts.

Creating Exposure

Participating, organizing, and hosting pop-up events is an essential sales and marketing plan. Businesses of all sizes and across various industries have been doing this for some time. With customers' needs and expectations constantly evolving, online businesses use pop-ups to generate buzz. Ways to seek and build product and brand exposure are by becoming well-known for the right reasons, excellent customer service, the solution to a problem, accessibility, going offline, purposefully connecting with people, and commitment to what I refer to as the 360-degree connection.

Becoming Well-Known for the Right Reasons – Participating in events and generating buzz are simple approaches for your company to become well-known within your community and industry. Being easily noticed because your business can reach and fulfill desires both online and offline is tremendous. Although running a company is not a popularity contest, being prevalent for the right reasons can attract customers to your pop-up shop. Furthermore, if you're not physically present at a pop-up, your audience can still visit your website through the QR code link they scanned while you operated at a venue. It doesn't stop there; loyal patrons may drive miles in inclement weather to your physical storefront in all seasons because you've also "*Popup Your Storefront*" months before and provided them with your brick-and-mortar store location.

Becoming well-known for offering excellent customer service, providing valuable solutions to customer problems, and ensuring accessibility are always goals worth striving for.

Excellent Customer Service – Excellent customer service entails providing high levels of support and assistance to patrons in a friendly, efficient, and effective manner. It includes a range of practices and behaviors aimed at satisfying the needs and expectations of customers. Creating a positive experience for your guests at pop-ups is required. This may include promptly and helpfully responding to inquiries, resolving issues, addressing frequently asked questions proactively, and anticipating potential problems.

A Solution to a Problem that Adds Value – A solution to a problem that adds value to consumers is a product, service, or approach that addresses a customer's need or pain point, enhancing their overall satisfaction. This type of solution not only solves the problem but also offers features, attributes, and benefits that improve the customer's life in some way. By demonstrating online and offline a deep understanding of people's needs and delivering a solution that exceeds their desires and adds value, you differentiate your offering from others in the marketplace. This builds customer loyalty and drives business growth.

Accessibility – Ensuring the accessibility of your business to customers is important for various reasons. It offers convenience and enhances the likelihood of customers engaging with your products or services, resulting in increased sales and revenue. Accessibility also plays a vital role in customer satisfaction by providing convenience and efficiency. Inclusivity is another aspect of accessibility, ensuring that all customers, including those with disabilities, can equally access and engage with your business. By catering to the diverse needs of your target audience, you demonstrate a commitment to diversity and inclusivity, expanding your customer base and gaining an advantage over online-only business owners.

Use People and Technology to Connect – Connecting with people in person and purposefully with technology builds exposure. "Waiting for people to find your business is not a strategy," as Russel Brunson from "ClickFunnels" aptly stated. Delegate your salesforce to engage with communities and sell with purpose. Pop-ups provide an opportunity for your brand to reach your targeted fanbase through word-of-mouth marketing on social media and offline. Furthermore, customers gain a deeper understanding and appreciation for your goods and services, and by connecting with them, you build trust and a good reputation.

The 360-Degree Connection – Ultimately, the goal is to create a 360-degree marketing strategy that effortlessly connects The Launchpads: digital realm (e-commerce), startup professionals, physical storefronts (brick and mortar), and side-hustle (hobby). This connection is facilitated using people and technology as the medium, with pop-up shops serving as the central hub or engine for growth. Regardless of the order in which customers engage with any of the launchpads, the key is to connect with each person who visits your shop and give them access to your business for future transactions.

Encourage customers to use their devices to explore your online business space and other areas of operation. Purposeful connection between shoppers and your sales force is vital, fostering brand awareness and ideally translating it into profits.

Go Offline – In basic terms, take your online products or services and physically present them to people, engaging their senses and offering a complete brand experience. Utilize creative imagination to design compelling pop-up shop presentations that articulate and display your brand story or message. This is how exposure begins to happen, and before you know it, your micro-to-small business can become one of the top merchants in your market segment. By going offline, you connect with real-world individuals, gaining insights and building exposure.

With these strategies, you can drive brand and product exposure, enhance customer engagement, and position your business for success.

Gain Insight into the Real Word

Gaining insight into the real world through physical experiences, pop-up shops make connections between your online business and the offline dominion. While your online popularity may be thriving, it's essential to consider how your business fares beyond the e-commerce space. By setting up temporary physical outlets in high-traffic areas or at sponsored events, such as local farmer's markets or themed festivals, you capture the attention of passersby and potential customers who may have never encountered your brand online.

Real-Time Customer Interactions

Insight into the real world helps us to uniquely engage with people on a personal level and understand their needs and desires in real time. By actively listening to customers' and having conversations with them at your booth, you become aware of what they are looking for and how your company can fulfill those needs. This direct interaction allows nurturing connections. Even small gestures like a smile or a wave can make a significant impact in forging lasting relationships.

Moreover, the real-world customer service experience provided by pop-ups enables you to identify what aspects of your business are working well and what areas may need improvement. By paying close attention to the conversations, you have with customers and actively seeking their advice, you can gather tremendous insights. These insights can guide your organizational decisions on pivoting, allowing you to adapt and refine your product offerings, services, and overall business approach based on real-world customer needs and preferences.

The information you gather from these interactions helps you understand the effectiveness of your current strategies and identify opportunities for growth and innovation.

Real-Time Competitive Analysis

In addition to understanding your own business, pop-up shops also gain a real-time understanding of your competitors. By observing and analyzing their activities during these temporary physical retail spaces, you can gather intelligence.

Pop-up shops allow you to observe your competitors' products, services, and customer interactions firsthand. By physically visiting their pop-up locations or closely monitoring their online performance during pop-up events, you can examine their offerings, pricing strategies, marketing campaigns, and customer engagement techniques. This direct exposure gives you a comprehensive understanding of how to position yourself, attract customers, and differentiate your brand.

Analyzing the behavior and responses of customers who visit your competitors' pop-ups provides additional insights into the strengths and weaknesses of their offerings. This real-time feedback helps you identify areas where you can improve.

Furthermore, engaging in conversations and interactions with customers at your own shop, also offers indirect insights into your competitors. Customers may share their experiences and compare you with those of your competitors. By actively listening to their feedback, you can gain deeper knowledge about what customers appreciate, dislike, or find lacking in your competitors' products or services. This information can guide you in refining your own offerings to better meet their expectations and outperform your rivals.

Pop-ups also lead to collaboration and networking with other entrepreneurs. Collaborating with complementary or non-competing businesses can open doors to new strategies, customer base, and market positioning. Sharing experiences and ideas with these businesses can spark creativity and perspectives on how to approach competition within your industry.

Also, in response to the growing online retail of brick-and-mortar businesses, it's important for e-commerce only business owners to develop a plan that works. Have you considered the potential of launching a pop-up shop as a means of exploring new markets?

While the popularity of online retail is undeniable, research indicates that many shoppers engage in online product browsing but ultimately make their purchases in physical stores. In fact, a Google survey reveals that 61% of shoppers prefer buying from brands with physical stores over those with a pure e-commerce presence only. Please recognize that by operating solely online, you may be missing out on a significant portion of your target market. Therefore, launching a pop-up shop presents a chance to tap into this market segment with low risks involved.

The beauty of employing pop-up shops for market testing lies in their versatility. They allow you to venture into unfamiliar markets where the response of your target audience remains uncertain. Since testing a new market involves a certain level of risk, a pop-up shop minimizes potential losses by limiting your investment specifically to that market. This way, even if the response is not as positive as anticipated, the financial impact on your overall business is contained.

Test New Markets – Studying Consumer Response

One of the primary objectives of market testing through pop-up shops is to study consumer response to a marketing campaign or a specific product/service. Engaging face-to-face with people at venues provides an unparalleled opportunity to gauge their responses in real time, as previously stated. By creating a tactile and engaging environment, businesses can observe firsthand how consumers respond. The gathered info helps with decisions on product improvements and adaptations. This ensures that the offerings align closely with the preferences and expectations of your target audience.

Furthermore, studying consumer response at pop-up shops opens new opportunities to access and fulfill the desires of customers. By closely analyzing their purchasing patterns, businesses can identify untapped needs and develop innovative solutions to meet them. This process can enable your business to pivot when necessary, optimize offerings, and establish a strong foothold in the market.

Create New Opportunities

Market testing is a multifaceted tool that not only evaluates consumer response but also uncovers new opportunities for growth. It acts as a gateway to untapped market segments, diversifying reach and revenue potential. Engaging with pop-up shop consumers and gathering feedback helps identify unexplored opportunities, broadening the customer base and tapping into new territories.

Additionally, market testing refines marketing strategies by understanding consumers' perceptions, enabling tailored campaigns to capture the desired audience's attention and loyalty.

In the face of rapid market evolution, market testing offers a strategic advantage, allowing your business to outmaneuver competitors by continually adapting and improving.

Moreover, if you are seeking growth and diversification, market testing is crucial for expanding into new markets. It provides insights and reduces risks associated with entering new territories, enabling informed decisions about resource allocation based on rigorous testing and analysis.

Research Brick-and-Mortar Locations

If you are aspiring to own a storefront, use pop-up shops as a tool for researching your brick-and-mortar location(s). This comprises a meticulous examination of various localities to gauge market potential before committing to a permanent storefront. To test new markets, identify brick-and-mortar locations that align well with your audience and overarching business objectives.

By thoughtfully selecting the right venues for pop-up shops, you are given a chance to connect and engage with a fresh customer base. Start by establishing a comprehensive plan that incorporates market research, thorough analysis of demographic data, and consideration of key factors such as local competition, consumer preferences, and prevailing market trends. These efforts also contribute to decision-making regarding the best locations for pop-up shop operations.

The deliberate placement of pop-up shops in these selected locations serves as a powerful validation and refinement of market testing endeavors. This propels business growth and steers expansion efforts in a promising direction.

Minimal Risk

High startup costs are one of the most significant obstacles for new companies. Entrepreneurs can test their business ideas to see if they are feasible without risking their savings. Pop-up shops are a way for online stores to get their feet wet in the offline world, and they're also a perfect avenue for existing companies to try out a new venue. It grants minimal risk. Try or experiment with things, and if it goes south, you won't lose anything. Second, it provides an overabundance of opportunities with zero risk factors. Hence, pop-up shops feel like a blessing because you can't do the same in a physical store. To start with a brick-and-mortar store, you may need to put a lot of money aside. Plus, the demands of running a storefront can be overwhelming for someone dealing with anxiety.

For many businesses, pop-up stores are a great way to test out the markets as you scale up. It is an ocean where you can experiment with new things and new cultures. They are perfect for exploring the waters of emerging countries because pop-ups have significantly lower financial investment. Certainly, the model is a low-risk way to gain momentum if you are an online-only retailer looking to branch out into offline sales or want to extend your brick-and-mortar footprint to new locations.

In essence, market testing assists with product development, marketing strategies, and tapping into growth opportunities. This systematic approach paves the way for new and exciting avenues of growth and success, empowering businesses to build unique journeys for their audiences that are exclusively offered by their brand.

Effective market testing can propel your company toward a future brimming with opportunities for growth, profitability, and sustained success.

Pivot When Necessary

Pivoting is an encompassing term that is an industry norm, and it was explained with examples in *"Popup Your Startup."* However, I will briefly provide a recap.

It refers to shifting to a new strategy that works better for you in the current environment. As you pivot perhaps online only to offline, the issues you face will change, but you must be prepared to pivot at every stage as your pop-up business grows. Pivoting allows you to identify and profit from new opportunities that you may not have recognized before, just like this one. It gives your business a new lease on life and brightens your outlook. Hence, you have decided to also meet your customers in person at pop-up shop venues.

You may have gotten a copy of this book if you are doing sucky online, are interested in meeting customers in person, are thinking of going online, are looking for growth opportunities, or are simply curious to study a new concept. If any is true, then you will eventually move toward or attempt a new direction. Pivoting.

So now that you are offline, your online shop is participating in many events and receiving firsthand valuable responses from customers. The information you receive is what you will use as a pivoting Key Indicator and Benefit (KIB).

Please note that not all feedback received requires immediate action. This advice, in many cases, becomes relevant only if a trend of responses is noticeable. The reason I say this is because consumers generally have formed opinions of all sorts that can be biased. Generally, though, count on their viewpoints to be correct, especially if it's coming from the masses.

After observing and being keen on a problem or potential anomaly that is shared by patrons or lingers within your operation and external market, always be prepared to pivot. Pivoting is inevitable, and it is sometimes needed without a moment's notice. It can be uncomfortable and nerve-wracking to pivot on the spot, but it is often necessary. Furthermore, become foreseeable to adverse possible outcomes by listening to others, research, and then form your own conclusions. The decision to pivot may require careful planning and thoughtful doing for a company to rise higher than ever before. The same way you carefully acted, bought my book or series, then thoroughly read them before pivoting to *"Popup Your E-commerce."* But of course, you must first objectively look at your company. Realistically, be truthful to systems and processes that do not work, but you have fallen in love with an idea that is potentially flawed. Then, ask yourself, patrons, and your team the difficult questions, and be open to any disheartening feedback that comes your way. Also, avoid neglecting the information you have obtained while performing extensive market research. Even if the research at the time primarily focuses on the e-commerce business. Perform a microscopic evaluation of your competitors and identify what their strengths and weaknesses are. With that in mind, here are three recommended methods for compiling data and using it to your advantage. They are: Set ego aside, get ahead and stay ahead, seek customers' guidance, then pivot, when necessary, in a better direction.

Set Ego Aside

A leader's ego can be the obstacle that interferes with rational thinking. Step back, anticipate, and address the deficiencies that are hurting or potentially may hurt the organization. So do not become obsessed with your novel ideas only. More so, be fixated on fulfilling the needs of customers and value your team's input.

For instance, if your e-commerce is not generating sufficient revenue and exposure, then this would be a perfect opportunity to pivot the business offline with the pop-up shop framework.

Another situation may be your pop-up salesforce has advised you that customers have been requesting a certain product or service. Set ego aside by listening keenly, then do your own analysis and resolve as best as you can.

Begin to take notes of this key indicator and make any business turnarounds, if any are needed, for overall success. Acclimate as required if something is not working and pivot in a better direction to stay ahead and get ahead.

Get Ahead and Stay Ahead

This is one way to achieve success, thrusting your business forward and maintaining the lead. Please adopt a proactive approach and continuously stay ahead of the curve. Disregarding or, even worse, procrastinating on the signs that call for action and adaptation can hinder your business from making progress and ultimately hamper its ability to keep its competitiveness. It is essential to recognize that in business, you must be as vigilant as a hunter in a jungle swarming with competitors.

The world is constantly evolving, with people's needs, societal shifts, and technological advancements progressing at an astonishing pace. With this rapid change, it has become increasingly important for businesses to possess the awareness and agility required to navigate the shifting tides successfully. The competitive arena is fierce, demanding that entrepreneurs and business leaders possess the skill set necessary to anticipate and respond to what lies ahead.

Therefore, to move your business forward and maintain a leading position, consider the following strategies:

Embrace Adaptation – Acknowledge the need to adapt to changing circumstances. Instead of resisting or avoiding change, view it as an opportunity to evolve and grow. Embracing new technologies, consumer demands, and market trends can position your company, from micro to large, at the forefront of innovation.

Foster a Learning Culture – Encourage a mindset of continuous learning within your company. Inspire employees to seek

SECRET GUIDE #1: UNDERSTANDING THE POWER OF POP-UPS

knowledge, explore new ideas, and develop new skills. By fostering a learning culture, you create a workforce that is better equipped to face challenges and seize opportunities as they arise.

Monitor the Pulse of the Market – Stay informed about the latest industry trends, consumer preferences, and technological advancements. Regularly assess the competitive landscape and identify potential disruptors or emerging players. By staying attuned to market dynamics, you can anticipate changes and act proactively.

Embrace Strategic Partnerships – Collaborate with other businesses and organizations that complement your strengths and fill your gaps. Strategic partnerships can enable you to leverage shared resources, access new markets, and tap into fresh perspectives, propelling your business forward.

Encourage Innovation – Adopt a culture that promotes innovation and experimentation. Encourage your team to think creatively, challenge the status quo, and explore new possibilities. By embracing innovation, you can stay ahead of the competition and consistently deliver value to your customers.

Leverage Technology – Embrace technological advancements that can streamline operations, enhance productivity, and improve customer experiences. Stay informed about emerging technologies relevant to your industry and evaluate their potential to drive growth and efficiency within your business.

Cultivate Customer-Centricity – Prioritize understanding your customers' ongoing needs. Regularly engage with your target audience, gather feedback, and tailor your business accordingly. By placing the customer at the center of your business plan, you can build strong relationships, foster customer loyalty, and drive long-term success.

Personalization is another aspect of customer-centricity. Tailor your products, services, and marketing efforts to align with individual customer likings. Use customer segmentation to create targeted campaigns and offers for a specific group. By providing a personalized experience, you make patrons feel valued and understood.

Moreover, prioritize exceptional customer service at your pop-up booths and online shop. Invest in training your staff to deliver consistent and empathetic support. Promptly address customer concerns, resolve issues efficiently, and go the extra mile to exceed expectations. A positive customer service experience can significantly impact customers.

Regularly evaluate your customer-centric initiatives to ensure their effectiveness. Track key performance indicators (KPIs) like customer satisfaction scores, customer retention rates, and repeat purchase rates. Use this feedback to refine and improve your strategies continually.

Adopting a customer-centric culture throughout your organization is vital. Communicate the importance of customer focus and empower employees at all levels to prioritize customer satisfaction. Encourage cross-functional collaboration to share customer insights and ideas. By aligning your entire team around the customer, you create a unified approach that delivers exceptional experiences.

By focusing on customer-centricity, you also further strengthen relationships, boost loyalty, grow customer advocacy, and drive long-term success. With these in place, you build a customer-centric culture that helps with decisions to pivot for growth.

Another effective way to build customer-centricity, as I previously described, is by actively listening to your customers and letting them guide you. By proactively seeking out and valuing their opinions, you demonstrate that their voices matter and that you are committed to meeting their needs.

Seek Patron's Guide – Getting feedback and guidance from your pop-up customers can be helpful when you're selling things online. Pop-up shop customers usually like local brands a lot, and the fact that they take the time to visit your temporary physical store shows they're really interested in what you're selling. This means their opinions and feedback are super important because they can tell you a lot about what they like, don't like, and what's popular right now. So, it's a good idea to find a pop-up location in your area and let your supporters be your guide.

Listening to what pop-up customers have to say helps to build a personal connection with them. Remember, they are another person; interact with them as such. You can collect their feedback through surveys, comment cards, or by talking with them directly. This helps you gather information about what they prefer, what products they'd like to see, and what problems they might have.

One cool thing about engaging with pop-up shop customers is that you can spot new trends and figure out where there might be gaps in the market. By watching how customers behave, what they buy, and how they interact with your products, you can get a real-time understanding of what's hot right now. This helps you see where your online business can step in and offer something that's in demand. Plus, analyzing their feedback can show you which products or features are popular, which is also great for planning what to sell next.

Observing how customers experience your pop-up shop is another way to get their guidance. Pay attention to things like how your booth is set up, how products are displayed, the level of customer service, and the route they take when navigating your pop-up stand. You can get a sense of how engaged customers are as they shop. If you notice anything that needs improvement, you can make changes based on customer suggestions. This constant improvement makes the shopping experience better overall.

So, the secret is out: appreciating pop-up shop customers' guidance gives e-commerce entrepreneurs a chance to make any necessary pivots. By listening to your patrons and seeking their guidance, you'll get valuable information that can help you make smart decisions as you navigate the world of e-commerce.

Pivot in a Better Direction

Now, let's probe into the concept of pivoting your business to steer it toward a more prosperous direction. In this exploration, we will uncover the significance of pop-up shops and their pivotal role in facilitating your transformative journey.

Whether your business is facing challenges, anticipating a potential downturn, or simply seeking ways to improve its performance, pivoting can be a strategic approach to steer your company toward a more profitable direction. One way to facilitate this pivot is through the utilization of pop-up shops, which can serve as catalysts for energizing your business growth while leveraging your online store as a launchpad for success. Pivoting in a better direction not only addresses significant problems but also acquires new customers and generates increased revenue.

One common challenge faced by many new companies is the lack of exposure. Despite having a fantastic product or service that fulfills a need in the market, they struggle to reach their target audience. To determine the direction in which you should pivot, assess the factors contributing to your business underperformance. This requires asking yourself some hard questions about various aspects such as pricing, product quality, packaging, or even the existence of a viable market.

To pivot successfully, it often involves shifting your focus toward a different vertical or a new set of customers. For instance, let's consider a scenario where your business previously catered to students who purchased snacks after school. However, with the ongoing global pandemic, in-person classes are no longer being held, leading to a decline in your customer base. In this case, a pivot might involve targeting a different market segment, such as delivering products locally to people working in businesses or homes instead.

Another aspect of pivoting is exploring new revenue models or adopting different technologies to improve your offerings. For example, if your business provides services for healthier snack selection tips, you could consider charging a small fee for the classes that were previously offered for free. Additionally, you might explore using new technology in the manufacturing process to create safer or more environmentally friendly products. By carefully planning these transitions, every business has the potential to pivot and achieve better performance.

Timing is also critical when it comes to pivoting. It's advisable to pivot early, especially when you realize that your current product or service is not gaining sufficient exposure or does not meet the market's needs. The goal is to improve your company's revenue or ensure its survival in the market. Even with a wealth of professional experience, you may have and a seemingly straightforward path to success, it's important never to take the process for granted and always be ready to learn and pivot based on changing circumstances.

As an online business owner, you may have been offering your products and services to customers for a long time. However, for various reasons, you may have decided to change certain aspects of your offerings, leading to what we now know as pivoting. But how can you ensure that this pivot doesn't negatively affect your business, especially in the online realm?

This is where launching a pop-up shop can be immensely beneficial. Whether you're shifting your target audience, aligning with your customers' demands, or aiming to boost sales, a pop-up shop provides an ideal platform to execute your pivot smoothly. Particularly if your online business is not thriving under its current model and you want to transition it to a brick-and-mortar setting, launching a pop-up shop can be the bridge that does that.

For example, if you're introducing changes to your business, such as shifting to technical and complex products like electronic appliances, a pop-up shop can serve as an educational platform to showcase and explain these new offerings to the market. This direct and tangible interaction with shoppers helps build trust and understanding, enhancing their willingness to engage with your updated products or services.

Pivoting your business in a better direction involves making shifts to address challenges, meet market demands, and improve overall performance. By deploying pop-up shops, you can effectively execute this pivot and ensure a smooth transition. Whether you're using a pop-up shop to gain exposure, target new customers, or educate the market about changes in your company, it serves as a powerful tool in facilitating growth and success during the pivoting process.

Bottom Line (Environmental Benefits)

When used creatively, pop-up shops help online businesses strengthen their brands with a bootstring budget. In addition to being cost-effective, they bring forth other worthwhile benefits.

As people become more conscious about their environmental impact, there has been a rise in outdoor businesses such as pop-up shops. Conducting pop-ups outdoors not only has the potential to generate more revenue but also has a range of associated environmental health benefits. In this section, I will briefly discuss the environmental health benefits of operating an outdoor business like a pop-up shop and why it is essential for e-commerce business owners who spend most of their time in front of a computer-centric device to market their products through pop-up shops.

Environmental Health Benefits of Operating Outdoors

In pop-up shops, where businesses move between indoor and outdoor spaces, there's a noticeable trend – more and more people prefer outdoor venues. In this shift, the benefits of operating outdoors for the environment are becoming clearer. This discussion examines the positive aspects of outdoor operations, focusing on how they improve air quality, reduce carbon footprint, and promote overall sustainability. As we explore these advantages, it becomes clear that placing these mobile shops outdoors provides a unique and engaging experience and creates a greener and more eco-friendly business environment.

Improved Air Quality – One of the primary benefits of operating a business outdoors is that it can significantly improve air quality. When you spend time outside, you are exposed to a higher concentration of oxygen, which can increase your energy levels and improve your mood. Outdoor spaces also have fewer air pollutants, including volatile organic compounds (VOCs), which are commonly found in indoor spaces.

Reduced Carbon Footprint – By operating an outdoor business, you significantly reduce your carbon footprint. Unlike traditional brick-and-mortar stores, pop-up shops do not require large amounts of energy to power heating, ventilation, and air conditioning systems. Additionally, pop-up shops have a smaller physical footprint, which means they require fewer building materials and generate less waste.

Increased Sustainability – Working your business outdoors can also contribute to increased sustainability. By operating a pop-up shop, you are encouraging people to spend time outside and support local businesses. Pop-ups also have the potential to create a community of like-minded individuals who are passionate about sustainability and reducing their environmental impact.

So, Why Pop-ups?

While e-commerce businesses have revolutionized the way we shop, they have also made it easier for people to spend most of their time in front of a phone, computer, or other smart devices. For e-commerce business owners, this can lead to a sedentary lifestyle and increased stress levels. By marketing their products through pop-up shops, e-commerce entrepreneurs can enjoy the environmental health benefits of spending time outdoors.

Increased Brand Awareness — Pop-up shops allow e-commerce business owners to showcase their products in a unique, stress-free, and memorable way, creating a lasting impression on potential outdoor shoppers. Remember, it can also be used to launch new products or test out new markets. For more on this, please review the prior information in the earlier section.

Improved Health and Wellbeing — Spending time outdoors has been linked to improved health and wellbeing. Being in nature can reduce stress levels, boost your immune system, and improve your overall temperament. By marketing your products through pop-up shops and e-commerce, you can prioritize health and wellbeing while still growing your company online.

Increased Sales — Pop-up shops have the potential to generate more sales than traditional brick-and-mortar stores. They are typically located in high-traffic areas, such as busy shopping districts, popular sponsored events, or tourist hotspots, which can attract many potential customers.

For those of you who spend most of your time in front of a smart device or laptop, marketing your products through pop-up shops can provide a much-needed break from the digital world and contribute to improved health and well-being.

By prioritizing outdoor business ventures, you create a more sustainable and fulfilling work-life balance.

The power of this new opportunity is essential for continuous e-commerce growth. A prevailing operation will always open infinite thoughts and imagination that are required for success. Next, use your newfound discoveries to support and define your company website's SEO strategy and central purpose.

THE POWER OF POP-UPS WORKSHEET –
Claim the Benefits.

1. List the Key Indicators and Benefits (KIB) of pop-up shops mentioned in the text.

_____
_____
_____
_____
_____

2. Which of these indicators and benefits do you find most relevant to your business, and why?

_____
_____
_____
_____
_____

3. Why is it important to avoid becoming too attached to your initial business ideas or strategies when considering a pivot?

_____
_____
_____
_____
_____

4. What are the benefits of observing your competitors' activities at pop-up shops?

_____
_____
_____
_____
_____

SECRET GUIDE #2
Website SEO and Central Purpose

Prepare Your E-commerce Business for Dream Customers.

As you read this section, attempt to refine your e-commerce website SEO with a well-defined purpose or value proposition. The previous secret has revealed the keys that opened ideas of how to best serve your audience. Now, use these insights to prepare and get ready to greet your dream clients online. If a lot of work is required for you to get up to speed, don't panic. Take baby steps daily and develop your site slowly and accurately. You will be happy with your efforts after realizing the results you will eventually see in as little as a few hours, with some changes and improvements if necessary.

Even if you feel that your e-commerce website is optimized with a well-defined purpose, I recommend that you thoroughly review the information that I have outlined in this secret. Then, you will have no issues driving any type of traffic (direct, organic, paid, social media) and convert, which I will show you how throughout this book. But first, let's analyze how to build and develop a website to capture and deliver the purpose of your product or services that will fulfill your pop-up shops and online customers' expectations.

PART I

Make Preparation

The objective is to prepare your business online in anticipation of an abundance of site visitors. These people are coming from offline pop-up shop QR code scanners, entering your business website and social media URL into their mobile devices. Others will visit your website via organic or paid search traffic to look for what you propose. Later in Secret Guide #5, "Direct Traffic to Your Online Brand," you will learn how to drive traffic to your e-commerce store and other online places.

Preparing your e-commerce and overall online business is done by defining a central purpose website. Additionally, a clearly focused and search-engine-optimized website information, structure, and design will greatly assist with delivering a lot of the right site visitors naturally or organically. This will be discussed further in this guide.

But as part of preparing for your website development, a few things must be met first.

The people or audience who land on your site pages generally fit into one of three desires they are looking to achieve from you. These desires belong to what are called the core markets of **Wealth**, **Health**, and **Relationships**. Hence, before building a focused and optimized e-commerce site with a defined central purpose, it's best to know and understand which core market/desire your dream customers fit.

Core Market Desires

The marketing concepts pertaining to well-being, affluence, and interpersonal connections have been deeply ingrained in the desires of humanity, and they boast extensive historical significance within the marketing community. Presented below is an overview of their relevance to you as an entrepreneur doing business online and offline. As you read to understand these core market desires, imagine how any of the three relates to your business.

Health – The yearning for robust health has perennially represented a fundamental necessity for human beings. In marketing, products and services that cater to health-related aspects have been promoted for countless years. However, the modern emphasis on health marketing gained substantial momentum during the 20th century, coinciding with the emergence of mass media and the flourishing wellness industry. By capitalizing on the aspiration for physical wellness, companies embarked on promoting diverse health products, fitness programs, dietary regimens, and healthcare services to consumers. *Examples of companies that align with this market desire include Johnson & Johnson, Fitbit, Planet Fitness, and Whole Foods Market.*

Wealth – The pursuit of wealth and financial prosperity has consistently acted as a driving force throughout historical epochs. In the marketing domain, the focus on affluence has grown alongside the fluctuations in economic systems. In bygone eras, advertisements often appealed to individuals' yearnings for economic wealth through products capable of enhancing their social status or improving their financial circumstances. With the advent of capitalism and consumerism, marketing endeavors expanded to cater to the growing ambitions for wealth accumulation and material possessions. In contemporary times, marketers persistently target consumers by accentuating how their products or services can contribute to financial success, security, and a lavish lifestyle. *Examples of companies that align with this market desire include Goldman Sachs, PSBI, Tiffany & Co, and Rolex.*

Relationship – Innately, we are social creatures, and the longing for relationships has consistently constituted a central facet of our existence. Within the marketing realm, the emphasis on interpersonal connections has transformed to mirror societal shifts and cultural values. In previous times, advertisements often depicted products or services as means to augment personal relationships or allure romantic partners. As society experienced increased interconnectedness, the advent of social media and digital platforms further underscored the significance of relationships. Modern marketing strategies frequently harness the yearning for connection, belongingness, and social validation to promote products, experiences, or platforms that facilitate social interactions. *Examples of companies that align with this market desire include Facebook, Starbucks, Airbnb, and Tinder.*

The historical roots of marketing concepts tied to well-being, affluence, and interpersonal connections run deep, shaped by humanity's desires and the evolving cultural landscape. While marketing strategies have evolved, these core desires remain lasting drivers of consumer behavior. As you contemplate how your business supports these desires, it's crucial to recognize that consumer desires can be perceived, actual, or both. For instance, someone may desire wealth and seek to project it by owning a Rolex watch, which represents perceived wealth rather than actual wealth. Yet, this perception may be sought to attract genuinely affluent individuals. Similarly, shopping at Tiffany & Co. may reflect a desire for perceived affluence. Conversely, companies like Goldman Sachs offer tangible paths to wealth for those seeking actual financial prosperity through a reasonable approach. Therefore, when considering how your company satisfies consumer desires, understand whether your audience seeks actual, perceived, or both forms of fulfillment in relation to these core desires.

These core market desires hold a central and indispensable role in the marketing strategies of diverse companies, spanning from micro-enterprises and small and medium-sized businesses to large corporations. Whether it's an e-commerce venture, a brick-and-mortar storefront, a side hustle, or a growing startup, these concepts remain pivotal in shaping successful marketing endeavors across the board.

At islsnac, my Caribbean Shopping Resort company, our primary focus is cultivating meaningful **Relationships** with our ideal customers. On the other hand, through my Pop-up Shop Business publications, seminars, and coaching programs, I aim to empower you to generate **Wealth**. Now, let me simplify each core market desire with a brief, straightforward explanation before telling my story:

Wealth: The innate longing to amass substantial financial resources or capital.

Health: The deep-seated desire to attain well-being by eliminating ailments or illnesses through the utilization of relevant products and/or services.

Relationship: The sincere yearning for acknowledgment, acceptance, the cultivation of love, unity, and genuine connections with others.

My Story

On the memorable date of May 4, 2019, I eagerly participated in my very first pop-up event, although its purpose and desired fulfillment were not entirely clear to me at the time. All I knew was that I wanted to explore the possibility of shifting from my underperforming e-commerce launch to doing pop-ups. It was a moment of courage, a step toward redemption, as I had grown tired of resorting to online strategies that yielded subpar results. These strategies included drawing for straws in the vast ocean of the internet, attempting lackluster SEO techniques touted by so-called marketing firms, and reaching out to Facebook users who merely liked and followed my posts without taking any further action.

In retrospect, I can't blame those Facebook users for their lack of engagement. Why would they bother clicking through to my website when there was no compelling reason to do so? My posts lacked direction, aimed at the wrong audience, and failed to resonate with anyone in particular. I will dig deeper into this issue in my next secret revelation, titled "Align Brand Message and Theme." It was a frustrating realization, but I was simply unaware of these crucial features. Hence, I made the decision to venture into the world of pop-ups for the very first time as an entrepreneur.

Taking swift action, I utilized the knowledge and resources I had at my disposal. My primary intention was to serve the Suffolk, VA community to the best of my abilities and, hopefully, make the islsnac brand desirable in the process.

To my delight, the pop-up event witnessed an impressive turnout of shoppers, many of whom were pleased to sample our specialty Caribbean baked goods and sorrel mocktail. However, I also noticed that while customers browsed and supported us, they yearned for more information. They wanted to understand why and how our products or services would fulfill their desires, if any. Essentially, they sought clarity on our purpose as a business. Thus, with each transaction, a flurry of questions ensued. At our booth, guests inquired whether our offerings were gluten-free, vegan, or healthy. I confidently responded with answers such as "No, it's not gluten-free" or "Yes, our sorrel drink and coconut drops are vegan-friendly." However, when it came to the question of whether our products were healthy, I found myself hesitating. I would say, "Hmm... Kinda... The sorrel mocktail is, but the bread pudding isn't gluten-free, and the sweet potato pudding can be prepared in a vegan style." The sheer volume of inquiries was overwhelming, and it became evident that every person who stopped by our stall wanted a valid reason to support our small local pop-up shop business.

Fortunately, we fared well, generating gross sales of $560.23 in just four hours, with minimal overhead expenses. It was especially exciting to discover that the venue we were sponsored by provided a canopy free of charge for the event. This was a fantastic bonus, as it offered much-needed shade that our small tent couldn't provide. Moreover, with the profits earned from that venue, I was able to purchase an extra canopy and two additional tables, leaving some money in the bank. I consider my first pop-up show to be a decent performance. Well, "decent" instead of "awesome" or "great" because I realized that the power of pop-ups could multiply in every aspect of our business if executed correctly. Furthermore, our revenue could have potentially doubled or even tripled had we focused on fulfilling a single core market desire, which I will discuss in the upcoming section.

Effectively delivering sales and marketing messages to individuals who share a common core market desire is far more impactful than attempting to cater to everyone's needs and pain points. Inadvertently, we were trying to appeal to the vegan interest market by offering coconut drops while simultaneously being unable to provide gluten-free baked goods. Both of these offerings likely fell under the umbrella of the desire of the healthcare market. Additionally, our sorrel mocktail, which sold out quickly, was positioned within the realm of relationship-building, as I had initially described it to my first customer as a nonalcoholic social wine substitute. Our presentation and preconceived FAQs were improvised because, at the time, our overall company's core market and purpose were not clearly defined. However, fast forwarding to the present day, we have come to understand that islsnac's taste vacation nostalgia nurtures the core market desire for cultivating relationships through the snacation experiences, both online and offline.

It is crucial to comprehend the desires of your target audience and utilize this understanding to craft a purposeful sales pitch, brand theme message, and relevant information for both your online and offline presence. By focusing on a single core market desire that resonates with your patrons, you can maximize your reach and provide the desired results they seek. Attempting to address multiple core market desires will only serve to decrease your effectiveness and limit your potential customer base. This would ultimately result in a significant reduction in potential revenue, which is something you certainly want to avoid.

Therefore, it is paramount to align your business strategy with a well-defined core market to unlock the full potential of your offerings and ensure the success of your pop-up shop business.

Submarkets and Niches

When considering the expansion of your business, do not only focus on core markets but also extend into submarkets and niches. To describe this, let's take the example of purchasing my book(s) with the intention of building overall revenue growth for your company. The desire you have as a consumer by investing in this book is wealth, which is the core market desire. However, there are various options available within submarkets and niches that cater to this desire.

For example, the submarket I am presenting to you can exist as either an online business or a physical storefront. These represent different avenues through which you can pursue your wealth-building goals by purchasing my books. The niche, on the other hand, refers to the specific platforms or locations where you can access copies. It could be the Amazon Kindle marketplace for online access or a physical bookstore like Barnes & Noble for a printed copy. Here, the submarket and niche act as the vehicle or path through which you obtain the desired results.

It is worth noting that while the submarket and niche may change, the core market desire remains constant. With my book offerings, I have the flexibility to switch from one submarket to another or from one niche to another while still addressing the same core market desire. As an example, the core market desire for wealth can be pursued through an online education submarket using Amazon Kindle as the niche or through a physical store submarket with Barnes & Noble as the niche.

Wealth (core market) – Online Book Store (submarket) – Amazon Kindle (niche)

Wealth (core market) – Physical Book Store (submarket) – Barnes & Noble (niche)

Furthermore, if I find that the submarket or niche I initially chose has become saturated with competition, it becomes crucial for me to brainstorm new opportunities. This entails exploring alternative ways of fulfilling the desired results for you, my audience. For example, if the online niche of the Amazon Kindle marketplace, serving as the platform for my pop-up shop business books, becomes highly competitive, I might consider exploring additional submarkets and niches. Participating in a Business Book Expo could be an option, with the submarket now encompassing Book Expos and the niche becoming physical pop-up shops selling books at a booth targeted at entrepreneurs like yourself. This strategic shift allows me to maintain my focus on the core market desire for wealth while venturing into new avenues for reaching my intended audience.

Submarkets and niches provide different paths and platforms to cater to specific desires within the broader core market. By understanding the interplay between these elements, you can position your business to effectively address your target audience's desires and remain adaptable in the face of competition or changing market conditions.

Wealth – Book Expo – Pop-up Shop Book Sale

Moreover, tactically positioning your business in a competitive marketplace is often referred to as discovering your "blue ocean," steering clear of intense competition or "red ocean" scenarios.

Blue Ocean, Red Ocean

"Blue Ocean Strategy" is a concept coined by W. Chan Kim and Renée Mauborgne in their book titled "Blue Ocean Strategy: How to Create Uncontested Market Space and Make the Competition Irrelevant." The book outlines a strategic framework for businesses to break away from the competitive pressures of traditional markets (referred to as "red oceans") by creating new market space where competition is irrelevant or minimal (termed "blue oceans").

In a "red ocean" scenario, businesses compete in existing market spaces, often leading to intense rivalry, price wars, and limited growth opportunities. On the other hand, a "blue ocean" strategy involves creating new market space by offering unique value propositions, innovative products, or services that fulfill previously unmet needs or redefine existing market boundaries. By doing so, your business can attract new customers, capture untapped demand, and achieve sustainable growth without direct competition.

The book provides practical tools and frameworks for identifying and navigating blue ocean opportunities, including the strategy canvas, the four actions framework, and the six paths framework. It emphasizes the importance of value innovation, which involves simultaneously pursuing differentiation and low cost to create a leap in value for both customers and the company.

Overall, "Blue Ocean Strategy" offers valuable information for businesses looking to strategically position themselves in competitive markets by creating new market spaces and unlocking uncontested market opportunities.

Now it's your opportunity to adopt the same approach as you aim to fulfill the desires of your potential audience. Explore submarkets and niches that provide you with a significant competitive advantage by finding your blue ocean and staying clear of bloody waters—your red ocean.

Analysis of Submarkets and Niches

Let's further discuss this in more detail using the example of a vendor selling organic skin care soaps for body healing. In this example, the core market is health, and the submarket revolves around organic skin care soaps. The niche, on the other hand, is focused on body healing, which serves as the specific path or vehicle through which desired results are achieved.

Health (core market) – **Organic Skin Care Soaps** (submarket) – **Body Healing** (niche) (path or vehicle to desired results)

By segmenting your marketing materials and information per this core market, submarket, and niche structure, you are effectively targeting individuals who desire healthy skin and are seeking organic soaps to heal their bodies and improve skin health.

As you progress through the subsequent sections, you will discover the value of this information when it comes to planning and organizing your SEO (Search Engine Optimization) efforts. Defining the central purpose of your business and website allows you to align your content with the core market desire, submarket, and niche you have identified.

Whether you operate a pure e-commerce website, a brick-and-mortar storefront with an online presence, or exclusively function as an online marketplace (such as Etsy or Amazon), the goal is to grow your business and reap monetary rewards by focusing on one core market.

For instance, wealth can be pursued through an online business model that encompasses online marketplaces like Etsy, eBay, or Amazon. Alternatively, it can also be achieved by establishing and growing your own e-commerce website using platforms such as Wix, Shopify, Weebly, WordPress, or Square Space, which also has tools to help you succeed. Additionally, another avenue for wealth creation can be explored through the framework of operating pop-up shops and utilizing the concept of "*Popup Your E-commerce.*"

Wealth – Online Business Tools – Online Marketplace (Etsy, Amazon)

Wealth – Online Business Tools – E-commerce Website

Wealth – Pop-up Shop Business Tools – Popup Your E-commerce

In the above example, the core market of wealth represents the overarching desire you want for your business. The submarket consists of various options, such as an online business or pop-up shop, which support your efforts in achieving wealth or financial freedom. You can leverage online marketplaces, establish your own e-commerce website, or embrace the framework of Popup Your E-commerce.

It's important to note that switching between these different submarkets and niches represents the acceptance of new opportunities that align with your desires. This information I am delivering to you now represents one of those new opportunities as you study this book in preparation for future application.

Understanding the relationship between the core market, submarket, and niche helps in targeting the right audience, optimizing your SEO strategies, and growing your business. By positioning your offerings and marketing efforts with the desires of your target market in mind, you can position yourself for success and achieve your desired financial results.

To offer further clarity on this subject, below are several examples that showcase core markets, submarkets, and niches.

Core Market	Submarkets	Niches
Wealth	Stock Market	Day Trading
Wealth	Online Business Tools	Run Google Ads to Website
Wealth	Real Estate	Flipping Houses, Rental Property
Health	Nutrition	Paleo Diet
Health	Weight Loss	Power Workout
Health	Skin Care	Organic Soaps
Relationship	Dating	How to Make a Good First Impression
Relationship	Parenting	How to Raise Teenagers
Relationship	Socializing	How to Overcome Shyness

By utilizing the worksheets provided, you will be able to effectively identify and complete the core market desire, submarket, and niche that your company offers. This exercise may lead you to perceive your company in a different light than before, as it prompts you to deeply consider the needs you are fulfilling for your target audience. It is important to note that there is no definitive right or wrong approach to how you satisfy and serve your audience's needs. What truly matters is having a clear understanding of the desires you are addressing.

Is your business primarily focused on building wealth, promoting health, or enhancing relationships? The crucial aspect is aligning your company's overarching purpose and message with the specific desire your company fulfills. This alignment ensures that your company's mission and the value you provide are congruent, leading to a more effective and impactful business.

Central Purpose

Explaining your company's central purpose and how you can add value to targeted individuals has to be done with care and precision. After understanding how you fill a core market segment desire, you can safely become laser-focused on what you speak of or write as it relates to your brand. This means that every piece of information and material that is broadcast across your brand locations online and offline must align. For that reason, I have divulged how to align the brand message and theme in Secret Guide #3 of this book.

Remember, the dream audience that is searching for what you offer must connect with you upon first encounter. Therefore, prepare well for their visit. Website guests in search of a specific solution must immediately know that your company's purpose of existence is to solve whatever problems they have. In some cases, they may not yet be aware they have a problem.

Defined Purpose Helps Overall Growth

If you have decided to make pop-up shops an extension of your e-commerce operation, there are a few important things you need to work on first. What I mean is ensuring that your online presence is viable and ready for the tremendous attention it will get. If the purpose is not clearly stated, then your overall business growth will be inconsistent. Placing limits such as misleading brand messages, inconsistent product offerings, unfamiliar images and color schemes, and other anomalies tend to create disconnects with your potential audience and will derail all your hard work. Doing it right the first time or after learning the right way laid out in this secret should be your goal.

Your e-commerce business is of very little use if it is just slapped together beautifully for the sake of just having a website. Hence, I have put together this guide for you to define your website and brand's central purpose, which helps you connect well with your dream customers. Essentially, your overall business must be defined to reach a targeted group of people based on their needs. I will show you how to make your website scream loudly to the folks whose lives you intend to change.

Once again, please read and reflect to see if your site needs updating and if it's designed and developed to receive visitors. I assure you that you will know what to do next after churning out this juicy information. I have incorporated a detailed guide on how to build or refine your website that provides clear, purposeful data with proper SEO strategies.

At the end of this Secret Guide, use the following questionnaire to help you refine your e-commerce website's SEO and define its central purpose. Reflect on your business and its alignment with core market desires, submarkets, and niches. This exercise will guide you in optimizing your website for your target audience. Answer each question to the best of your ability.

PART II

Search Engine Optimization

Search Engine Optimization (SEO) is a vital component of en-suring that your website effectively reaches and engages your tar-get audience. To achieve this, you must adopt a detailed and me-thodical approach that speaks directly to your audience and leaves no doubt that they have arrived at the right place. This process begins with a thorough understanding of the people who intend to do business with you, which is established by iden-tifying your core market desire, submarket, and niche. Once you have this foundation in place, you can build upon it to attract a specific group of people.

Deliver Focused Data, Structure, and Design

A well-focused approach that caters to a specific group of cus-tomers is one of the key factors in achieving success in e-com-merce. Knowing your audience is required as you create relevant and engaging content. Furthermore, develop an effective website structure and design a suitable user interface.

Central to effective SEO is organizing your website structure and implementing a practice known as siloing. This falls under the umbrella of On-Page SEO, which will be discussed in detail later in this section. Also, before you read any further, I encourage you to pause momentarily and familiarize yourself with a widely used SEO jargon called "ROCKET," as it serves as a guide throughout your SEO endeavors.

Our partners at Crawlfrog SEO services highly recommend us-ing ROCKET as a tool to best serve our clients. It's good for you to know this too. For more information on Crawlfrog SEO, check out their website at www.crawlfrog.com.

Rocket

Rocket is an acronym that summarizes important activities in the field of SEO that can significantly improve a website's search engine rankings and visibility. Each letter represents facets of SEO that you, as an e-commerce business owner and marketer, should focus on to effectively operate online.

Let's explore each letter in the "ROCKET" acronym:

Research: This involves conducting thorough keyword research to identify the most relevant and high-traffic keywords for your website. It entails understanding your target audience, analyzing competitors' websites, and identifying keyword gaps and opportunities.

Optimize: Once you have identified your target keywords, the next step is to optimize your website's content and structure to enhance its relevance and authority for those keywords. This includes optimizing on-page elements such as meta tags, headings, and content, as well as off-page elements such as backlinks and social media presence.

Content: The quality and relevance of your website's content play a role in SEO success. Creating high-quality, original, and engaging content that aligns with your target keywords and audience is an important part of any SEO strategy.

Keyword: Keywords serve as the foundation of your SEO strategy. By identifying and targeting the right keywords, you can attract the appropriate audience to your website and improve your search engine rankings.

Earned media: Earned media refers to the publicity or exposure that you gain through media relations, content marketing, social media, or other digital marketing efforts. Earned media can enhance your website's visibility, credibility, and authority in the eyes of both search engines and users.

Testing: Testing and monitoring your website's performance is needed for ongoing SEO success. By analyzing website data and user behavior, you find areas for improvement and refine your SEO strategy over time. Tracking and analyzing your SEO efforts through rigorous testing will be covered in Secret Guide #9.

By prioritizing these elements throughout the development and maintenance of your website, you will stay grounded in what truly matters. Implementing the ROCKET approach will help improve your website's search engine rankings, increase visibility, attract more traffic and leads, and ultimately achieve your business goals. Therefore, always keep SEO marketing at the forefront of your mind. Nevertheless, before making updates to your website using ROCKET or starting a website from scratch, pre-planning and organizing are prerequisites to ensure smooth and successful execution.

Preplanning and Organizing

This book is specifically written for entrepreneurs who are primarily involved in operating an online business or have plans to start one, with the growth engine being pop-up shops. If you fall into this category, the next step is to prepare an inventory of assets that will either build from scratch or enhance your existing website.

It is understandable that you may have dedicated months or even years to building a website that aligns with your vision in terms of appearance, functionality, and overall experience. Therefore, the goal is not to undermine the effort you have put into it. Gathering and acquiring inventory assets will greatly assist you in making any necessary adjustments to support your pop-up e-commerce endeavors.

At this stage, preplanning and organizing with a creative and open mind are of utmost importance. Understanding how your website functions, its features, and its overall appearance is instrumental in the optimization process. It's now time to start brainstorming potential resources that will prove beneficial as you plan and strategize.

Gathered Assets

The process of gathering assets for your e-commerce venture includes a varied range of materials that you have created or accumulated within your niche. These include brochures, flyers, photos, reviews, videos, logos, images, product prices, articles, manuals, tutorials, and customer correspondence. Every piece of information that has the potential to contribute to crafting relevance and attracting your website visitors must be considered.

These gathered assets form the core ingredients for your recipe for online success. By examining the materials your business has already produced or intends to create, you can significantly enrich the overall content and enhance the user experience. Each asset holds the potential to engage your audience and provide a clear picture of your products, services, and brand story.

Moreover, these assets wield tremendous power when it comes to your keyword research strategies. By analyzing and leveraging the existing assets, you can uncover keywords and phrases that support your target audience's search intent. These keywords will not only enhance your website's visibility in search engine results but also facilitate a deeper understanding of your customers' needs and preferences.

Incorporating these gathered assets into your e-commerce journey will bolster your online business and elevate your brand's credibility and authority. With a wealth of relevant and engaging materials at your disposal, you create a comprehensive and compelling user experience for your site visitors.

Acknowledge the potential of your collected resources and let them guide your path in planning and organizing.

Keywords and Keyword Phrases

These are the building blocks of effective online content and SEO. By understanding what these terms mean and grasping their importance, you can boost your business online.

Keywords serve as a connection between users and search engines, helping search algorithms understand the relevance of your web pages to specific queries. Another term, *Keyword Phrases*, on the other hand, are longer combinations of words, also referred to as long-term keywords, provide a more precise context for your content.

Now, why are keywords so crucial? Well, they act as signposts that guide search engines and potential visitors to your website. By including relevant keywords in your content, you increase the likelihood of your pages appearing in search results when users search for related topics. This leads to increased organic traffic and better overall visibility.

However, it's not enough to simply choose a handful of keywords and call it a day. It is imperative to verify the keywords you plan to use or are already using for your website. Verifying your keywords confirms their relevance and popularity among users. If your list of verified keywords is less than fifty, it is highly recommended that additional research be conducted to ensure a robust keyword strategy.

Expanding your keyword repertoire can be highly beneficial. The more keywords you research and use, the better your chances of capturing a wider audience and attracting more potential organic site visits. Please make sure that these keywords are incongruent with the expectations and desires of people within your core market, submarket, or niche. This alignment will enhance the relevance and resonance of your content with your dream audience.

In the upcoming sections, I will explain more about keyword research, sharing detailed explanations and practical strategies to help you uncover the most viable keywords for your website. Stay tuned for tips and techniques to refine your keyword strategy and achieve greater online success.

As you work on creating your list, I'll provide a basic example scenario.

Suppose an individual is browsing the internet in search of organic skincare soaps to cater to their sensitive skin and promote overall body healing. They might employ search terms like "natural soap for sensitive skin" or "soap for body healing." Consequently, it's essential for this site owner to incorporate these two keyword phrases into their compilation of 50. However, it's worth mentioning that the main keywords or phrases you include must undergo validation for effectiveness using various tools such as SEMrush, Ahrefs, Moz, Google Keyword Planner,

Answer the Public, and Keyword Everywhere. Use whichever of these tools you are comfortable with.

An overview of at least one of these tools, which pinpoints high-volume and low-keyword-difficulty (KD) keywords, will be provided in Secret Guide #9 of this book. Also, follow the worksheet example at the end of this secret to manage your keywords effectively.

Your list of main terms, keyword phrases, or search intent questions should affiliate with what your targeted audience may enter on search engines like Google, Bing, or Ask.com to potentially find your business. It is important to remember that people are browsing the World Wide Web in search of solutions to their needs and areas of concern. They, we, are seeking ways to address or improve wealth, health, or relationship difficulties, and your website must be competitively built to rank for keywords associated with one of these core markets.

To be competitive in searches, your website's on-site SEO efforts will require effective implementation of siloing, structured data, content relevance, and consideration of site visitor intent. This will likely position your website on the first page of search engine results pages (SERPs) for most of your key terms.

The knowledge gained from this section will prove helpful as you preplan and organize. However, before probing further into my SEO strategies and actively working on your site, I will take the time to explain SERP as much as I can.

SERP

Understanding SERPs and their features will greatly assist you in your keyword research endeavors. It is an easily accessible tool that serves as a benchmark for your expected ranking and aids in analyzing direct and indirect competition.

Google and other search engines provide users with the Search Engine Result Page (SERP). At first glance, the SERP interface may not appear overly complicated, considering the trillions of people worldwide who rely on Google SERP to access the information they desire. However, there is more to understand about SERP than meets the eye.

Even though most of us are familiar with using Google or Bing to search, the Search Engine Result Page is a complex and multilayered ecosystem. That's why you must pay attention to it and grasp the basics. Being aware of what appears on the SERP is essential for website owners, whether they are managing their SEO or utilizing the services of an SEO firm.

This knowledge can make a significant difference in either boosting the chances of driving traffic to your site or jeopardizing the efforts.

Let's take a closer look at what Google SERP specifically offers and how it can impact organic traffic to your website.

Organic Results

The fundamental component of SERP is organic results. These are the listings of websites that Google and other search engines display in response to a search query. They are referred to as organic because the websites listed in this section do not pay for their placement on the SERP. Please note that when an entity pays for visibility on the SERP, it falls under the category of paid search. Organic results appear because Google believes they are the most relevant matches for a specific keyword based on numerous factors. When scrolling through the SERP, organic results are easily identifiable by the inclusion of the page's URL, a clickable title, and a brief description of what can be found on the corresponding webpage.

But it's worth noting that the appearance of organic results may evolve over time. In older versions of Google's organic results, especially, the page's URL was displayed in green font above the title. So, anticipate potential changes in the appearance of organic results in the future.

Furthermore, organic results may have a slightly different appearance on mobile devices. The most noticeable difference is the inclusion of a favicon, which is a small icon associated with a website's URL. Favicons are typically displayed in a browser's address bar or next to the website name in a bookmark list. When creating a website, it is advisable to upload a favicon, as it adds a professional touch and enhances the overall presentation of your business on the SERP.

Rich Organic Results

Another type of result that Google introduces on the SERP is known as rich results. Rich results can include various additional information and even visual elements. Moreover, Google may feature useful sections from well-optimized web pages as rich results. Conversely, there are methods to transform your organic results into rich results. Website builders like Wix employ techniques that involve using a script called "Structured Data Markup," which is added to the backend of your webpage. The good news is that reputable software, including those provided by Google, can generate the necessary markups for you. By utilizing these markups, you can create rich results such as article previews, product previews, and frequently asked questions (FAQs) for your webpage's search results.

Structured Data Markup Tools
https://www.google.com/webmasters/markup-helper/
https://technicalseo.com/tools/schema-markup-generator/

Rich results offer several advantages over regular organic results. They tend to occupy more space on the SERP, making them more noticeable and potentially attracting more clicks. Rich results can incorporate visual elements like carousels, images, and other non-textual content. Some rich results may also display review stars and image thumbnails. Imagine if your webpage were the only one on the SERP with these elements—its visibility would immediately stand out. Conversely, if your site lacks these elements and others have them, it could be more challenging for your page to capture attention and attract visitors.

I hope that exploring SERP and understanding organic results has inspired you to act. Remember, you can achieve your goals by optimizing one page at a time and committing to the journey. Before you know it, your web pages could be ranking on the first page for most, if not all, of your targeted main keywords. However, the examination of SERP features doesn't end here—there are other features at your disposal.

SERP Features

Imagine everything we've covered so far about SERP, and yet, we've only scratched the surface. In addition to organic results, there are several other SERP features that Google incorporates into the results page. These features enhance the user experience by providing additional information or directing users to new content.

In addition to our current understanding, let's now discuss a few other SERP features. These features are designed to enhance the user experience by providing relevant and diverse information.

There are five common types of SERP features: Paid SERP Features, Navigational SERP Features, Organic Opportunity SERP Features, Non-Organic Opportunity SERP Features, and Local Searches and Knowledge Panels.

Paid SERP Features – Paid SERP features include prominently displayed advertisements on the search engine results page. These ads are typically marked as "sponsored" and are often positioned at the top or side of the page. Advertisers bid on keywords relevant to their products or services to ensure their ads are displayed when users search for those terms. Paid SERP features provide businesses with the opportunity to promote their offerings and effectively reach their target audience.

Navigational SERP Features – Navigational SERP features are designed to assist users in navigating to specific websites or web pages directly. These features commonly include site links, site search boxes, and breadcrumbs. Site links are additional links displayed beneath the primary search result, leading users to specific sections or pages within a website. Site search boxes enable users to perform targeted searches within a particular website, while breadcrumbs provide a hierarchical trail indicating the path users have taken on a website.

Organic Opportunity SERP Features – Organic opportunity SERP features include elements that offer an opportunity for organic search results to rank highly and attract user attention. This includes traditional organic search results, which are non-paid listings that appear based on their relevance to the search query. As

I explained earlier, search engines rank these results using algorithms that consider factors such as keyword relevance, content quality, and backlink profile.

Non-Organic Opportunity SERP Features – Non-organic opportunity SERP features include elements that do not provide an opportunity for organic search results to rank prominently. Examples of such features are featured snippets, knowledge graphs, and answer boxes. Featured snippets display concise information extracted from webpages at the top of the search results, providing users with quick answers. Knowledge graphs are panels that offer structured information about specific entities, such as famous people, movies, or historical events. Answer boxes provide direct answers to user queries without requiring them to click on any search result.

Local Searches and Knowledge Panels – Local searches and knowledge panels are SERP features specifically relevant to location-based queries. Local searches display a map with your business listings and related information, allowing users to find nearby services, restaurants, or storefronts. Knowledge panels, on the other hand, provide detailed information about entities, such as businesses, landmarks, or public figures, often sourced from trusted databases like Wikipedia.

As you can see, understanding SERP involves recognizing the complexity and layers it encompasses. From organic results to rich results, paid features to navigational features, organic and non-organic opportunities, and localized elements, the search engine results page is obviously very diverse and dynamic. By familiarizing yourself with these different features, your decisions in the optimization of your e-commerce website will help to improve its visibility and attract targeted organic traffic.

Moving forward from our discussion of SERP features, let's explore another aspect of optimizing your website for search engines: On-Page SEO. While SERP features determine how your website appears on the search results page, On-Page SEO focuses on optimizing individual web pages to improve visibility and relevance. It involves various techniques such as optimizing meta tags, incorporating relevant keywords, enhancing content quality, improving page load speed, and ensuring mobile friendliness. By employing effective On-Page SEO strategies, you can further enhance your website's chances of ranking higher in organic search results and attracting free organic traffic.

Here are the key elements of On-Page SEO and how they contribute to your overall SEO efforts.

On-Page SEO

SEO is an all-embracing term that has many variables. My goal is to cover the relevant material in this book. Understanding SERP is an example of one variable with other knowledge-building block topics. Most of what you will learn about Search Engine Optimization will guide you through a step-by-step process. You will gain tremendous organic site visits, i.e., free-flowing website traffic. Eventually, you will garner a compounding effect of brand exposure, with traffic also coming directly from pop-up shop venues.

I am passionate about coaching entrepreneurs like yourself with this information for your online business. With my experience as an SEO and Digital Marketing specialist, I have concluded that developing a proper On-Page SEO almost guarantees your business on page one of SERP. This means this is not the only criterion but the one that you have the most control over, and if done well, the results are impactful. In addition to On-Page SEO, there are Technical SEO, Off-Page SEO, and Local SEO. Before reviewing all SEO types coming up later, let's take the time at this junction to focus on the one you have the greatest control.

On-Page SEO involves the efforts that you put forth on your site structure, silo, and page content. This means properly optimizing your website title tags, headings, page content, meta tag descriptions, and keyword meta tags of each site page. It also means how your website topics or themes (main and sub) architect is designed with internal page link building.

Additionally, it comprises how keywords or keyword phrases are used for those topics or themes. If this seems confusing, the next section will further describe these terminologies.

As you further organize and plan your website inventories and list your top 50 potential keywords, it's now time to implement siloing tactics to effectively deliver your website's SEO and central purpose. Following siloing guidelines, I will also discuss in detail main-pages, sub-pages, SEO structure, linking, and the other three SEO types (Technical, Off-page, and Local).

Siloing

Siloing involves categorizing core keywords or keyword phrases into main page themes and sub-page themes for a website. This is followed by appropriately grouping and connecting pages with similar themes using both internal and external linking. This sums up the essence of siloing, which might seem challenging initially, particularly if it's your first encounter with the concept. However, with practice and creating your own silo chart, understanding it will become more manageable. Now, let's explore the concept of siloing and its potential advantages for your e-commerce website.

The silo SEO feature is used while planning your website page's topics and overall theme. It is the arrangement of your site according to the business service, products, and ideas you offer. These arrangements must be made using something referred to as subject/theme silos. For example, if your overall website offers a niche product/service that caters to "body healing," one of your subject or theme silos may be "organic skin care soaps."

Along with organic skin care soaps, you may offer body moisturizers and natural lip balms. Your site may also include training blogs on how to care for your skin. Furthermore, this online business owner also does pop-up shops, which is essentially referred to as *"Popup Your E-commerce,"* and are known as a body healing pop-up shop vendor that pops up at many neighborhood events.

These are examples of a subject or themed silo. Subjects (themes) must be arranged independently and not jumbled or spread out in pieces over several website pages. Avoid mixing these subjects together, with no order of emphasis. The goal is to have Search Engines classify each web page separately and not as one whole. Separating these subjects into their own area (website pages), they will be classified in their own areas (pages) on our example website as organic skin care soaps, body moisturizers, natural lip balm, skin care training blog, and body healing soap pop-up shop vendor.

The problem is that most websites never clarify the main subjects on the website pages they want to rank for. Instead, they try to be all things to all people. Each area (page) of your website must explicitly state the themes and keywords or keyword phrases used. Search engines consider a site with multiple pages of unique, informative content with designated main themes with supporting sub-themes highly relevant and useful. I will discuss later the relationship between main and sub-themes.

If done correctly, the results create prime search engine optimization. The siloing process helps categorize your web pages and subject/themes to group related content or information. This allows for your website to have a clear and straightforward topic relevance that will signal to search engines that you are a subject matter expert in your niche.

However, there are a few nuances to siloing that can make it complex. For this book, I will provide an intermediate breakdown of how to silo your website that beginners and pros can follow.

To begin, you need to select a main theme for your website that aligns with your online business. What does your business primarily focus on? For example, if a business revolves around promoting physical well-being, it may choose a main website theme like "body healing" or "body therapeutic." The choice between these themes depends on two factors:

> ➤ The theme that best captures the aspirations and desires of its core target market in the context of this ongoing example.
> ➤ The theme that is frequently searched for on search engines each month.

Considering that this website caters to the health needs of its ideal audience, the submarket and niche can be identified as skin care products and body healing, respectively. As "body healing" or "body therapeutic" represents the specific area that delivers the desired outcomes, the overall theme of the website should reflect that.

Also, this business must determine which niche, either body healing or body therapeutic, is searched for more frequently on search engines each month. To ascertain the niche phrase with the highest search volume, you can utilize keyword research tools such as Google Keyword Planner, SEMrush, Ahrefs, or others previously mentioned.

The point is to begin the siloing effort first by identifying and defining your website/business purpose big picture themed niche, followed by main themes and sub-themes with main keyword phrases assigned.

As you can see, your e-commerce site must generally have a big-picture idea that's comprehensive. This overarching theme is typically assigned to your website's homepage, which serves as the primary platform to showcase what you offer to your target audience. The homepage, along with the landing pages, should possess an irresistible quality by reflecting the core desires of the market, submarkets, and the specific niche that addresses the desired outcomes of your customers.

For instance, if "body healing" is the headline of this example homepage, identified as the main keyword phrase through research, the main heading (H1) could be crafted to say something like "Organic Body Healing Skin Care Soaps." This can be followed by an H2 subheading that emphasizes "Products for Sensitive Skin." I will provide further insights on headings later.

By adopting this approach, you present a unique value proposition to individuals seeking solutions to their problems. These two phrases, prominently displayed on this homepage, will also be effectively communicated by your sales team during pop-up shop events, featured on banners, and disseminated across various online channels, including social media platforms and online marketplaces like Etsy. I will share more details on this in the next Secret Guide.

Reading my guidelines on how to arrange your site to build a silo is an important lesson to learn as an e-commerce business owner. But before going any further, use a writing object and jot down some relevant information using the worksheet provided.

Please use this worksheet to reinforce your understanding of Search Engine Optimization (SEO) concepts discussed in the provided information. After reading the information, answer the following questions and complete the tasks to enhance your knowledge and apply it to your e-commerce website.

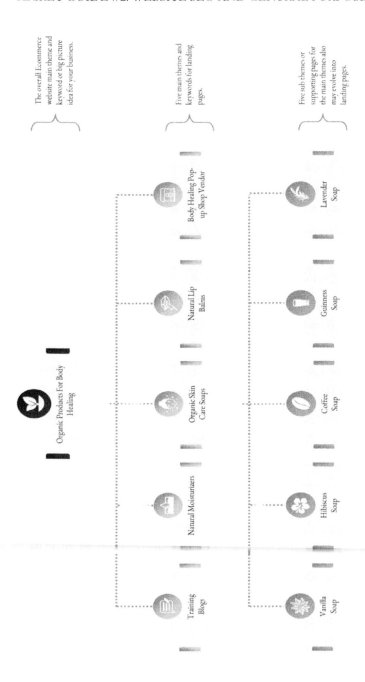

The overall E-commerce website main theme and keyword or big picture idea for your business.

Five main themes and keywords for landing pages.

Five sub themes or supporting pages for the main themes also may evolve into landing pages.

Organic Products For Body Healing

Body Healing Pop-up Shop Vendor

Natural Lip Balms

Organic Skin Care Soaps

Natural Moisturizers

Training Blogs

Lavender Soap

Guinness Soap

Coffee Soap

Hibiscus Soap

Vanilla Soap

Figure 1. Example silo chart.

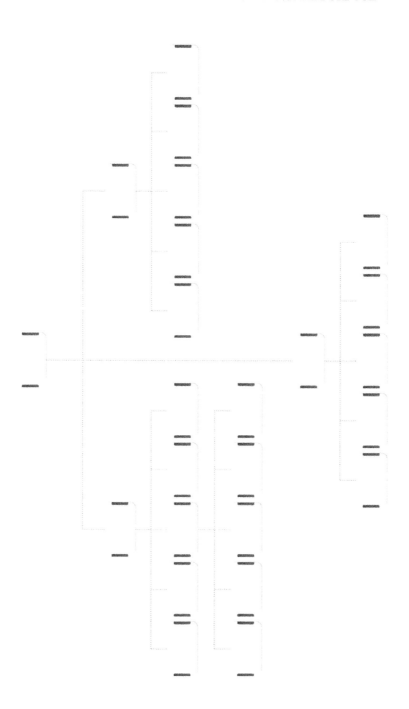

Figure 2. Fill in the boxes and create your own silo structure. Not all boxes necessarily need to be filled except for the website's main big picture theme at the very top and at least one of the main themes and subthemes. It depends on how many topics you want to cover in your e-commerce business. Start off with the basic product pages, blogs, and a page highlighting your pop-up shop venues. And, of course, the homepage.

PART III

Search Engine Optimization *cont.*

By now, you may be contemplating the optimal way to organize and optimize keywords for your website's pages or how to assign an overarching theme to your homepage. I will provide a more detailed explanation of this topic later. Firstly, there are four types of pages you must become familiar with: the main page or landing page, sub-pages, product pages, and article pages. These pages form the foundation of your silo design strategy. Additionally, the homepage, which represents your niche theme, also functions as a landing page.

Main Pages (Landing pages)

These are pages you want to direct your users to visit and do something, such as sign up for your newsletter, research information, or make a purchase. Landing pages contain the main subjects or themes that are supported by smaller sub-pages. Furthermore, the most valuable landing or main page on your website is the homepage, which captures your business and website overarching big-picture niche idea. Generally, in most cases, a homepage landing page will receive a lot of traffic (direct, organic, paid, and social media).

In e-commerce marketing, a landing page is sometimes referred to as a "Lead Capture Page," "Squeeze Page," or a "Destination Page." These main designated pages on your website appear in response to clicking search results on Google SERP, direct traffic from pop-up shop QR scans, marketing promotion, or email marketing to the email contacts list you own. For this section, I will primarily discuss landing pages as they relate to organic traffic due to effective On-Page SEO with proper siloing practices.

The landing page's role is to make an outstanding first impression on your ideal customers, leaving a lasting impact. They establish an immediate connection with your target audience by effectively addressing their core desires in relation to your business. These pages are purposefully crafted to inform, educate, engage, and ultimately convert visitors into satisfied customers. Additionally, they serve as a guide, leading potential clients to do as requested, such as signing up for your enticing online promotions.

Typically, a website consists of one or more landing pages, each supported by at least five sub-pages, such as articles, blogs, or product pages. These sub-pages are strategically optimized with primary keyword phrases. I will delve further into these sub-page types in the section on Site Page Structure. However, before going into those details, continue reading for a deeper understanding of how the main pages function.

Main Page Function

Each main page or landing page on your website must have a unique keyword or a set of closely related keywords or phrases. If you assign the same main theme keyword to two separate landing pages, search engines will only prioritize one of the pages and disregard the other. To avoid this, it is essential to make your landing pages distinct by focusing on a single subject or theme with a unique main keyword and related keywords. This approach should also be reflected in the content provided on those pages. For further guidance on this matter, please refer to the section on Keyword Research Strategy. Paying attention to this is of utmost importance.

Let's refer to our example of an online business focused on body healing. If you look closely at the main landing pages, you will see that they are optimized with carefully researched keyword phrases. These phrases include "organic skin care soaps," "body moisturizer," "natural lip balms," "skin care training," and "pop-up shop body healing vendor." The homepage, as expected, is dedicated to the overall theme of the website, with the keyword phrase "body healing." Furthermore, in the preceding paragraphs, I have provided a headline (Heading 1) titled "Organic **Body Healing** Skin Care Soaps," which incorporates the targeted keyword phrase. If you're feeling a bit confused about writing headlines, don't worry. I'll explain it in detail in the upcoming section.

If your designated landing pages are effectively optimized to attract organic traffic, your target audience has a higher chance of clicking on the link displayed on the search engine results page (SERP) when searching for specific main keywords. This click will lead them to a webpage that provides relevant information or matches their search intent, offering a solution to their needs.

Figure 3. Our example homepage represents the overall theme of this website, with an emphasis on "body healing." The headline displays, "Organic Body Healing Skin Care Soaps," featuring the keyword phrase "body healing" within

the H1 tag. Below the H1 heading, an H2 tag follows, declaring, "Organic Products for Body Healing."

Along with these main pages are sub-pages that you will learn about as you read on. Below, I have created a written silo example. Please build out your silo using the worksheet provided.

Example Silo Structure for Organic Body Healing Skin Care Soaps:

Main Category Page, i.e., Homepage:

Create a primary category page specifically for "Organic Body Healing Skin Care Soaps." This page will act as the main hub for all subcategory pages and associated content. This page is designated as the homepage, introducing the advantages, ingredients, and characteristics of organic body-healing skin care soaps. The page appeal is then enhanced with clear descriptions and high-quality images for user engagement.

Subcategory Pages:
a. Benefits of Organic Body Healing Skin Care Soaps:
Dedicate specific subcategory pages to showcase the advantages of including organic body-healing skin care soaps and other related products offered in the customer's routine. Elaborate on how these soaps and other body products effectively nourish, moisturize, and naturally heal the skin. These informative pages can serve as engaging blogs, informative articles, or impactful product landing pages. Also, incorporate relevant keywords throughout the content while optimizing meta tags and headings for enhanced visibility.

b. Ingredients of Organic Body Healing Skin Care Soap:
Create ongoing subcategory pages exclusively focused on exploring the components of organic body-healing skin care soaps. Each ingredient is provided, stating its advantages and its role in enhancing skin health and lifestyle changes. Here, page visibility is also enhanced with relevant keywords and enriched with high-resolution images and videos showcasing this information. This page can also serve as a blog for skincare enthusiasts.

c. How to Choose the Right Organic Body Healing Skin Care Soaps:
This is a subcategory page that guides users on selecting the most suitable organic body-healing skin care soap for their specific needs. Outline important factors to consider, such as skin type, ingredients, scent preferences, and product certifications. The aim is to optimize this content with relevant keywords while providing you with valuable internal or external links to recommended product pages on an e-commerce website or outbound to an online marketplace. Additionally, this topic lends itself well to a blog page that explains step-by-step instructions on "how to" accomplish something.

Product Pages:
a. Individual Organic Body Healing Skin Care Soaps and Other Products:
Individual product pages will be created for every variant of the organic body healing skincare line, which includes soaps, lip balms, and moisturizers. Each page should contain comprehensive descriptions, detailed product specifications, customer reviews, and high-quality images. Enhance the optimization of these pages with specific keywords that are relevant to the scent, size, ingredients, and distinctive features of each product in the case for this example.

b. Bundles and Gift Sets:

Create separate product pages for bundles or gift sets that include organic body-healing skin care soaps. Showcase the combinations available and emphasize the value and savings customers can enjoy. Include relevant keywords and optimize meta tags to attract organic traffic.

Body Healing Soap Pop-up Shop Vendor Category:
A dedicated main category page is created exclusively for the "Body Healing Soaps Pop-up Shop Vendor." This page will serve as a resource for pop-up shop vendor services, including hosting events, collaborations, and promotions at pop-up venues. It will provide customers with information on how to contact your company, the advantages they can enjoy, and the online ordering process with merchandise pickup options at different events. To enhance the page's visibility and relevance, again, include relevant keywords pertaining to pop-up shop vendorship, distinctive offerings, and the launching of new products.

Blog Section:
a. Skin Care Tips and Advice:
Here, a well-curated and engaging blog section will feature helpful articles that focus on skincare tips, expert advice, and do-it-yourself (DIY) recipes. These articles discuss natural body healing skin care soaps with compelling topics like "10 Essential Tips to Integrate Organic Body Healing Soaps into Your Skincare Routine" or "A Guide to Selecting the Perfect Organic Body Healing Skin Care Soaps." These blog posts not only serve as valuable readers and guides for blog visitors but also function as subcategory pages, expanding the scope of your website and showcasing industry knowledge and authority.

b. Product Reviews and Comparisons:

Compose detailed product reviews and comparisons that center on organic body-healing skincare soaps. Thoroughly assess various brands, scrutinize their ingredients, gauge their efficacy, and delve into user feedback. Enhance these articles by using pertinent keywords to entice prospective purchasers.

The provided breakdown of a silo structure serves as a foundation for organizing your website. It's important to note that you don't have to implement all components simultaneously. Begin with the homepage and gradually expand to include product pages. Even if you don't currently plan on having a blog or a pop-up shop vendor page, it's advisable to create a silo structure that allows for their potential inclusion in the future.

The construction of landing pages matters to search engines (Bing, Google, Yahoo) and helps them determine the relevance of each page of a website. The engines count everything that qualifies, like the total number of words, the content relevance, the intent of the page, how many times your main keywords are repeated on the page (prominence), and so forth.

And no, this is not one of Bing or Google's tricks that many struggling website business owners often allude to. Instead, it pays to make your page construction align with what Google considers optimal for each of these elements as much as possible.

Now that you understand how main pages work, list possible main theme landing pages associated with your overall brand niche. The number of landing pages that you list may depend on what you want to highlight in your business. It is also determined if the main or subcategory theme pages contain high-volume search main keywords. Also, remember that your silo main pages usually must satisfy your audience's core market desires.

SECRET GUIDE #2: WEBSITE SEO AND CENTRAL PURPOSE

Subcategory Pages

These contain the supporting information for your main theme or landing pages. Remember, all landing pages need at least five sub-pages of data to support them so they can be regarded as landing pages. As a rule of thumb, the five sub-pages that support the landing pages should be about a related topic or subject. The way to connect the subcategory and main pages is through internal page linking on your website. Interestingly, these sub-pages may evolve into landing pages themselves if they have enough supported material, i.e., again, at least five sub-pages of their own. These sub-pages are linked to a main page, with internal linking, which constitutes them a sub. Also, if the criteria are met as outlined above, then they will be referred to as both sub and main pages. Next, provided are three types of landing pages that you will have on your website.

Product Page – Please consider optimizing your product pages to serve as potential main pages. If you offer a product that has a relatively high search volume, such as thousands of searches per month, it would be beneficial to create a dedicated product landing page. Initially, this page may have been a sub-page

By optimizing a product page in this manner, you can provide more extensive and relevant information, as well as effective call-to-action features. However, it's important to note that product pages are often constrained by the layout limitations of most website builder platforms. They must also be designed around specific subjects or themes and utilize keyword phrases that attract potential buyers.

Therefore, it may not be necessary to exceed a word count of 700, as this could be excessive for a product page that aims to engage shoppers. I recommend aiming for a minimum of 500 words but no more than 700. A product title, brief description, shipping information, and well-placed call-to-action buttons may be sufficient for a product page. Considering the limitations of product landing pages, it would be wise to create an article page as well.

Article Page – Furthermore, you may decide to create a main page in an article form. In this case, use a different keyword, such as "skin care soap," with a much higher traffic volume of 50k monthly. In this instant, a dedicated article landing page is used, which again may have been a sub-page. This researched, recommended article main page must be optimized with the main keyword being "skin care soap." Therefore, you will assign this page a lot of relevant information with the main keyword and related keywords allocated in the tags with internal links, as well as incoming links or backlinks. Don't freak out, I will make sure to go over tags and linking, which is required after siloing. Stay tuned.

Article pages written similarly to blogs include photos, videos, and featured products on the pages. These pages are especially great for lengthy content that may be daunting to read. The criteria of content on your website are one that search engine bots take notice of. Meeting good content creation criteria will be explained next, followed by linking. Along with content, placing interactive features will keep your readers engaged. Articles usually contain lots of text and are an excellent place to have concise information for online researchers and smart shoppers.

Additionally, upon completing this article page, a call-to-action (CTA) button or link will be placed at least twice, usually at the top of the page before your customer scrolls. If your site visitors are glued to your site page material, assign a call to action at the bottom. They will have the option to act without scrolling up. This CTA text hyperlink or button will then direct your site visitors to the actual vanilla skin care soap product page or any other associated product page to possibly convert into a purchase. Speaking of purchases, try to highlight your pop-up shop operation for visibility and engagement on your website.

Pop-up Shop Page – Pop-up shop operation information must be included as a landing page dedicated to showcasing your offline activities, i.e., a page that shares information about all your events, such as a pop-up calendar, new venues, or promotions. Refer to the silo example guidelines I outlined earlier.

Now that you have built up your site pages or at least the themed landing pages, get ready to build out the structure and link building. Website structure and proper linking are mighty crafts for mastering following siloing.

Site Page Structure

When it comes to the structure of your website, there are several parts to it. These include the quality and quantity of content, effective keyword usage, different content types, and placement of keywords throughout various places, such as title tags, meta descriptions, heading tags (H1-H6), and paragraphs.

In this section, I will go over the entities that contribute to the page structure of your website. So, let's begin to uncover the key components that shape your site's framework.

Content

Content must be authentic, informative, valuable, relevant, intentional, and helpful to your website visitors. Your content plays an important part when it comes to ranking well on search engines. Using my content writing strategies will help drive traffic to your website and keep your visitors engaged. Even better, it will convert your casual visitors into loyal customers.

Like humans, search engines can "read" website content, but their understanding is based solely on complex algorithms. Unlike us, search engines cannot comprehend text in the same way. However, website optimization assists with providing search engines with clarity regarding the content we offer. By employing a well-defined optimization formula, you enhance search engines' comprehension of the various types of information that you present on your website. Knowing this now brings me to the topic of content types, which I will now discuss.

Content Types – The choice of content for your website depends on your specific website objectives. This guide is specifically designed to assist you in generating online revenue while establishing yourself as a subject matter expert in your respective industry. Therefore, I have discovered that it is highly beneficial to create a website that has both e-commerce features and research-based content. As you develop your content strategy, consider creating blogs and articles that cater to researchers while also offering products or services for potential buyers.

It is important to offer a balance between informative resources and purchasing opportunities. Ensure that your e-commerce platform includes blogging capabilities and a wealth of information. This can encompass various topics such as recipes or instructional blogs ("how to" articles). Additionally, include product and article pages that showcase merchandise available for purchase. Consequently, your keyword selection and research should cover two distinct paths: informational and transactional. This will enhance the relevance and intent of your website pages.

Relevant and purposeful content is crucial for catering to the specific intentions of website visitors. Intent refers to what potential visitors are seeking to obtain from your online business. It could be making a purchase, gathering information, commercial interests, or navigating to a specific destination within your website. Each page's content should be crafted to fulfill one of these intentions based on what you aim to achieve with that particular page.

For instance, a blog providing instructions on creating organic skincare soaps serves the purpose of delivering informative content. On the other hand, a product page that is fully optimized as a landing page aims to attract traffic with the intention of generating sales.

Content takes on several forms, such as product pages, articles, and blogs, utilizing words, videos, and photos. It's important to note that search engines are unable to decipher the information within an image or video. Therefore, it is advisable to use alt text to name and describe images and videos. Alt text not only assists individuals with hearing impairments in accessing web content, but it also supports search engine optimization efforts.

Quality and Quantity of Content – The quantity and quality of content required to stay competitive vary across industries. Search engine algorithms possess advanced capabilities. They examine the intent, relevance, quality, and quantity of your content by crawling your website pages and matching them with relevant search queries.

As a general guideline, it is advisable to create a minimum of 700 words for each website page whenever possible. When it comes to articles and blogs, aiming for a word count of 1500-2000 is preferable. Remember, the more comprehensive, the better, regardless of the industry. By surpassing the benchmark numbers set by your competitors, you can establish yourself as a leading industry expert and authority figure. If you feel that aiming for a word count between 700 and 2000 seems excessive, rest assured that it is not.

Once the words are incorporated into your website pages, they will naturally be distributed in places such as page headings, product descriptions, videos, illustrations, call-to-action buttons, and images. Consequently, after designing a homepage or landing page with, for example, 700 words, the overall word count may not appear overwhelming. However, blog pages typically feature 1500 words or more, and the extensive nature of the information should be managed by incorporating engaging videos or images to enhance readability. I will discuss blog writing techniques in a later section.

It is important to note that content length alone is not the sole criterion for achieving high rankings. Paying close attention to providing relevant content that aligns with visitors' intent is critical. It is imperative to utilize tools like SEMrush or Ahrefs' keyword overview to analyze the questions and queries people pose. Your task is to provide answers and intentionally deliver relevant information through a substantial amount of content that adds value to your website visitors. Revisit the section on "ROCKET" to keep you grounded in these optimization rules. Furthermore, in terms of having blogs on your e-commerce website, ensure that your blog categories support with your overall brand message.

Blog Content Categories

Having categories in a blog is important for several reasons:

Organization: Categories help to organize your blog content into relevant groups or topics. By dividing your content into categories, you make it easier for your readers to find the information they are looking for.

Navigation: Categories provide a clear and easy-to-use navigation structure for your blog. They allow your readers to browse through your blog and find the content that is most relevant to them.

SEO: Categories can help with search engine optimization by making it easier for search engines to understand the content and structure of your blog. By using relevant and specific categories, you improve the chances that your blog will appear in search results for specific keywords.

User Experience: By providing categories, you make it easier for your readers to find and consume your content, which can improve their overall experience on your blog.

Content Planning: Categories also help with content planning and organization. By identifying the key topics or themes you want to cover in your blog, you create a content plan that ensures you are covering all the relevant areas and providing value to your readers.

Overall, having categories in a blog is a tool for organizing, navigating, and presenting your content to readers in a way that is easy to understand and consume.

Content Writing Guidelines

Up to this point, I have given you enough strategies to get started with content writing. But how do you make the most of what you have learned thus far? While there's no one-size-fits-all approach, below are some rules to follow.

Write for people, not search engines – Think about your audience. What are they looking for? What do they want to know? The top secret is structuring your pages and content in a way that answers their search-queried questions. Make your content original and high-quality and provide value.

Use your keywords strategically but naturally – In the past, there was a lot of emphasis on using keywords wherever you could. But with my on-page SEO strategies, use your keywords according to my direction, as explained in the "Exact match main keyword distribution" section of this book.

Headings and subheadings must be clear and concise – Give readers enough info about each section on your page so they can quickly scan to see content relevance.

Use heading tags (H1-H6) – These tags give structure to your pages by dividing content into sections. Plus, they're vital for accessibility and SEO.

Creating fresh, insightful, and authentic subject matter topics – There are plenty of ways to do this, like blogging. As I have mentioned, blogs are highly effective for growing organic traffic. They attract new visitors and can drive conversions. Hint: do blogs.

Once you have read the section on landing pages and site structure, please complete the following worksheets to assess your understanding and guide your optimization efforts.

E.A.T

There are no shortcuts to building a well-optimized, content-driven e-commerce website. Invest time in creating high-quality, substantial content. That way, you're more likely to answer a variety of search intents, signaling that your site is relevant and valuable. If you are ever in doubt after doing all I have shown you so far, follow the acronym E.A.T, and your content will undoubtedly rank well.

E-A-T is an acronym that stands for Expertise, Authority, and Trustworthiness. It is a concept that has become increasingly popular in SEO content writing, particularly in the wake of Google's "Medic" update, which focused on the quality of content in the health and wellness industry.

Expertise – Refers to the level of knowledge and skill that a content creator has in their field. To demonstrate expertise in your content, it's important to share accurate and reliable information and to cite sources where appropriate.

Authority – Denotes the level of influence and respect that a content creator has in their industry. This is demonstrated through things like awards, recognition, and a strong social media presence.

Trustworthiness – Refers to the level of reliability and credibility that a content creator has with their audience. This can be demonstrated through things like positive reviews, testimonials, and endorsements from other trusted sources.

In SEO content writing, it's important to demonstrate E-A-T to build trust with both search engines and users. By providing high-quality, authoritative content that demonstrates expertise, authority, and trustworthiness, you can increase your chances of ranking well in search results and building a loyal audience.

Google started emphasizing E-A-T (Expertise, Authority, and Trustworthiness) in SEO content because it wanted to improve the quality of content that appears in its search results. In recent years, there has been an increase in the amount of misleading or inaccurate information online, particularly in the health and wellness industry. This has led to concerns about the reliability of information on the internet, and Google has taken steps to address these concerns by prioritizing high-quality, trustworthy content.

Google's algorithm updates, such as the "Medic" update in 2018, have placed greater emphasis on E-A-T as a ranking factor. This means that websites and content creators who demonstrate expertise, authority, and trustworthiness are more likely to rank well in search results. By promoting high-quality content and rewarding trustworthy sources, Google aims to provide users with the best possible search experience and ensure that they can find reliable, accurate information online.

Moreover, along with E. A. T. rules, it is essential to ensure that the content on each page is thoroughly optimized with your selected primary keywords. This optimization will ultimately result in increased organic website traffic, providing a valuable and cost-effective means of attracting visitors.

Keyword Strategy

Having relevant content and using appropriate keywords are both required when it comes to optimizing your website for search engine traffic. Keywords are the words or phrases that individuals use when searching online. It is important to understand and utilize keywords effectively to ensure that search engines can identify the relevance of your website's content while still making it readable and valuable for users.

There are methods you can employ to incorporate the main keywords into your web pages. These keywords should accurately represent and convey the essence of your page. By doing so, you provide search engines with noteworthy information about your content. It is recommended to place the keywords in multiple locations on your page to guarantee that search engine bots recognize them as representative of the page's content.

When designing and constructing web pages, focus each page on a specific keyword or a group of closely related keywords. This is a suitable opportunity to select and group relevant keywords or keyword phrases from your initial list of at least 50. These keywords or phrases are useful as you organize your website into main pages and supporting subcategory pages, supporting your overall website structure. Aim to use at least five supporting keywords per page, which can also be utilized to enhance the depth of your content. By employing supporting keywords, you can create at least five sub-pages, resulting in a fully optimized landing page. If necessary, you can revisit and review the section on landing pages for more details.

It is important to know that each web page should target a specific keyword or a group of related keywords and phrases. This in turn enhances the importance of each keyword. Avoid using the same keyword excessively on every page, as it can lead to what is known as keyword density. When search engines detect repeated usage of exact words across multiple pages on your website, they assign greater significance to the page where the keyword is used sparingly. Furthermore, having too many unrelated keywords with high rankings can dilute the theme or subject of your pages, thereby negatively impacting your ranking.

To tackle this, a simple solution is to focus on relevant high-volume main keywords with a low keyword density (KD) score. Strategically distribute these keywords with an exact match throughout their dedicated, well-optimized main or landing pages. Also, place the keywords in appropriate tags, as I will explain in the next paragraph.

Exact Match Main Keyword Distribution

The information provided below is suitable for creating content ranging from 700 to 2000 words or more. It is important to maintain a balanced approach and avoid excessive use of keywords, as search engines penalize keyword stuffing. The writing should flow naturally and appeal to website visitors. Instead of forcefully including the main keywords or phrases, it is advisable to ensure that they fit seamlessly into the written material. To distribute the main keyword evenly across a page with 700 or more words divided into five or more paragraphs, the following guidelines must be followed:

- Include the main keyword once in the title tag.
- Include the main keyword once or twice in the description Meta tag (in the HTML code).
- Include the main keyword once or twice, up to four times in the keywords Meta tag (in the HTML code).
- Use the main keyword once in the H1 tag (visible to users) within the text content.
- Begin the first sentence of the first paragraph (visible to users) with the main keyword.

- Use the main keyword twice within the first 200 words, including the first sentence.
- Include the main keyword once in paragraphs two, three, and four.
- Include the main keyword once or twice in the last paragraph.

Throughout these placements, it is important to use the main keyword as an exact match phrase. Search engines typically look for exact phrases when responding to search queries. They also consider the proximity and meaning of the words within a phrase, as well as different word forms (e.g., customize instead of customization). While writing your content, these characteristics are often naturally incorporated. However, intentionally placing the main keyword as an exact match phrase will increase the chances of your website ranking high on the SERP.

Apart from keyword management, search engines like Google also consider the following factors related to on-page SEO:

- Web pages that have all the terms of the phrase closely related in meaning.
- Web pages containing all the words, even if they are not necessarily close together.
- Web pages that include different forms of the words.

When following the outlined steps, there is a high possibility of ranking within the top ten on the SERP for your main keywords. However, achieving a top-five or top-ten ranking requires additional strategies beyond on-page SEO. Factors like backlinking, off-page SEO, technical SEO, and local SEO are also factors. Nevertheless, focusing on on-page SEO is a starting point, even if search engines modify their algorithms. To align your website with the mission of search engines, aim to create useful and accessible content that adheres to their guidelines.

To optimize the content for your e-commerce web pages, including blogs and landing pages, it is important to tactically put relevant keywords into various tags and sections. By carefully considering your page themes for siloing, you effectively enhance keyword relevance and accuracy. Ensure that exact match phrases are assigned to appropriate tags such as the title tag, description tag, keyword meta tag, H1 tag, and paragraphs. It's best practice to maintain keyword consistency throughout the content. Pay special attention to the placement of keywords in the title, description, meta description, keyword meta tag, H1, H2, H3, H4 tags, and the body content. By following these practices, you create content that is optimized and aligned with search engine requirements.

Title Description Tag

So, what is a title tag, and what role does it have in on-page optimization? A title description tag is visible on search result pages. It is the first thing people see when searching the internet for products, services, or content, such as blogs and articles. If your title doesn't match what people are looking for, chances are they will click on something else that closely matches their queried searched key phrase.

Along with seeing these tags on SERP, title tags are also seen while surfing on a web page or website, in the tab section. To see an example of a title tag, hover your mouse cursor on one of your website tabs while you surf the web using a laptop or tablet. You will notice a dropdown box that shows brief descriptive information. Every page on your website must have a title of 50-70 characters, regardless of the page's purpose.

Additionally, when you search on search engines, a list of relevant results will appear as snippets. This clickable bolded sentence is the title. In addition to what you learned earlier in the SERP section, snippets also include a URL and page meta description.

Your title needs to be fewer words than the meta description and quickly convey what a specific page on your site is about. This helps search engines get a better understanding of that page, increasing the chances that people will make a purchase, book a service, read your blog, and so on. Below are five listed hard title tag rules that you must follow.

Five Title Tag Rules:

- Each site page needs to have its own unique title. Be specific and make sure it reflects your page content. At first glance, it should briefly and immediately convey what to expect from that page.
- It is imperative that you include relevant, with intent, keywords, or phrases you want to rank for.
- While you can be descriptive, avoid multiple keywords—or keyword stuffing. The one way that I have used to bypass keyword stuffing is by combining keywords that form a perfect sentence. This sentence must be readable by people and identifiable by spiders or bots. If done well, search engines will not regard it as keyword stuffing. The same concept applies to your description, H1, and paragraphs. If two key phrases are simply slapped together without forming a proper sentence, people, as well

as search engines, will think it's spam. This can impact traffic to your site and may even hurt your ranking.

- If you're targeting local traffic, include the city and state you service. This is helpful for local SEO ranking locally for your business. If you had one location in Virginia Beach, VA, you would add it to your title. Even if you are an online store shipping to multiple cities, I recommend naming a geographic location you serve in the title. This needs to be done since you are now moving your online business to offline Pop-up shops in various areas of your locality.

- Include your brand or business name. This is about building brand awareness. You want people to make the connection between who you are and what you do at first glance.

Keep titles between 50-70 characters – Titles more than 70 characters will likely get cut off by search engines. Also, the length of title characters depends on what your competitors use for some keywords in your niche. For example, if competitors are ranking in the top ten with a max character for a specific key phrase, then you will perhaps need to make an adjustment. Do the same for key phrases in titles that are ranking well with less than 70 characters. A great tool to use to analyze this is SEMRUSH, or simply do a search for a key phrase on Google to see the top five results on SERP.

Remember, SEO is an ongoing effort, so go back and analyze assigned key phrases and test new ones to further optimize your titles if required. Do this even after your site is published and live.

Meta Description Tag

Just like your title tag, your page meta description displayed on search results is a chance to grab the attention. These tags appear below your page's title tag description on SERP.

The goal of a meta description is to provide a relevant summary of a specific web page. The meta description is lengthier than the title, with more details of what is to be expected in your page information. It must be written to attract potential customers and convince them your site has what they're seeking to find.

Think of it as your pitch; it should focus on what your page is about, what it intends to give, and the value you bring to web searchers. People, Google, and other search engines read this tag to catalog your site pages. Define clearly what each page is about with your primary keyword included. The secret here is to duplicate the title information as written in your title tag, plus additional info.

Description meta tags also define the name, purpose, author, and date of web pages. In some instances, it is also helpful to mention the country, state, or city that your business is in. This is particularly important for your homepage, which signals to search engines which part of the world your company operates.

At times, search engines will automatically adjust descriptions for your site based on your page content and what people are searching for. Therefore, even if you possibly wrote a killer description, Google may pull a sentence or two from your page content and display it on SERP without notice or your permission. This means that any one of your pages can show various descriptions depending on the search query people use.

As an e-commerce website owner, it's an SEO best practice to write your own meta descriptions. After all, you are the subject matter expert at what you do and should be one of the top industry leaders. At the least, attempt to be. No one understands your page content materials like you do, even if you decide to outsource your SEO projects. Whether you do it yourself or outsource, below are four recommended meta description rules.

Four Meta Description Rules

Create a unique description for each site page – Make sure your descriptions reflect the content of your pages so potential visitors know what to expect. No page should have the same meta description, the same as your other tags.

Make your descriptions engaging and actionable to potential website visitors. While descriptions should reflect your site pages, remember you're talking to people. Think about what will motivate them to click on your site, buy a product, or book a service.

Use your keywords or phrases with the right intent – If your description includes keywords matching a given search query, these words will appear bold in your description on SERP. This can increase the chances of people clicking through to your site. Use your best judgment and only use keywords when they reflect your page's content and intent. For example, if your meta description includes an actionable word such as "buy now online," the expected site page must display a product or service available for purchase.

Lastly, keep your descriptions short and to the point – Industrywide, it is recommended to have under 160 characters in your descriptions so they won't get cut off on the results page.

Remember, it's all about being a good match for what people are searching for. Invest time in your meta description. Every page counts in your SEO efforts.

Keyword Meta Tag

The keyword meta tag differs from other mentioned tags as it remains hidden from human viewers and is only visible to search engine bots. When creating these tags, it is advised to refrain from exceeding four mentions of the main keyword for a specific page within the tag script.

> **Example:** <meta name = "keywords" content = "how to make organic soap, organic bar soap, organic hand soap, organic soap base, organic soap">

In the given script example, the main keyword "organic soap" appears three times within the keyword meta tag. To reach the recommended maximum of four mentions, any additional relevant keywords or keyword phrases associated with organic soap should be included. This example serves as a simple and comprehensible keyword phrase and keyword meta script, as shown in my previous pop-up shop series. It can be particularly useful for those interested in the growing abundance of natural soap pop-up merchants.

Furthermore, I suggest utilizing the SEMrush tool to identify keywords with high monthly search volumes and low KD scores. When writing the script, arrange the keywords within the opening and closing tags in descending order from longest phrases or words to shortest. As a general guideline, it is advisable to place the main keyword phrase as the last item on the list. In this case, "organic soap" is the final keyword listed.

Moreover, the total number of keywords or phrases should not exceed ten. In this example, I have provided only five keywords or related keywords. Going beyond ten keywords or including more than four main keywords within this tag may be perceived as keyword stuffing by search engines, which must be avoided.

Headings (H1-H6 tags)

Heading tags in your website's HTML code represent the headings, ranging from H1 to H6. They serve as prominent titles or sections, like the headlines of a newspaper. These big topic headlines are often noticed by visitors more quickly than other page components.

The H1 heading tag is the primary heading and functions as the page title. H2 and H3 are secondary and tertiary headings, respectively. Depending on the depth of the content supporting the main H1 tag headline, pages can go up to H6. These tags follow a hierarchical structure, with <H1> (Heading 1) being the highest level and <H6> (Heading 6) used for sections and subsections within a page.

Computer programs assign more importance to headlines than regular page text. When using heading tags, it's important to be specific and concise with the heading information compared to the title tag. The main keywords in the title, description, and meta tags should also appear in the H1 tag (page headline). Each headline on your website pages should be unique and have its own set of heading tags (H1 to H6), if applicable. In essence, all pages on your site should have distinct main keywords.

Keep in mind that the primary keyword or keyword phrase designated for a web page should be included within the H1 tag.

Based on my experience with heading tags, I personally recommend using different heading tags for your titles. This enhances the structure of your pages, dividing them into section titles (H2) and sub-sections (H3). While you can use all six H tags to create in-depth content, I suggest limiting it to a maximum of four unless your material requires more than four sub-topics. However, this rule is not set in stone, especially if your content necessitates additional sub-topics. Below is a brief overview of the primary, secondary, and tertiary heading tags:

H1: The main headline of a web page. Each page should have only one H1

H2: A secondary headline or subtopic of the primary headline (H1). An H2 tag is not necessary if there are no subtopics for a specific page

H3: A subtopic that follows the H2. An H3 is not needed if no subtopics are required.

Headings help visitors understand the content of each page and contribute to search engine optimization. Before concluding this section on headings, I want to share something to be aware of, and that confused me for a while before I noticed it.

Heading Tag Caution

While building your heading tags, pay attention to line breaks. Make sure that there are no empty line breaks that are not designated a 'Heading 1' text theme. The same applies to the other heading tags when used. Instead, set the empty line breaks as paragraphs or an alt text image since that is usually the normal flow of page content, from top to bottom.

This mistake will automatically generate a blank H1 tag, indicating to crawling spiders that there are two lines of H1. You don't want that!

Paragraphs

Crafting a compelling opening sentence on a webpage serves as a concise preview of all the information presented. The conventional approach involves using "Paragraph 1" as the preferred format for conveying the content. It is crucial to incorporate the main keyword, which appears in the page title tag, description tag, meta tag, and H1, within the first sentence of the introductory paragraph. Consequently, it becomes imperative to establish distinct landing pages with exclusive keywords and content information. This holds tremendous significance as it influences the decision of users who, upon searching for these distinct keywords, are more likely to click on the link displayed in the SERP. Subsequently, they will be directed to a page that furnishes pertinent information corresponding to their search. In addition, having secondary keywords on these pages is beneficial, yet the primary objective remains the creation of focused content with accurately placed main keywords in the title, meta description, keyword meta tags, H1, and paragraphs.

Linking

Linking is another key player in SEO and website optimization. I see linking, if done correctly, as the tool that ties it all together and serves to signal communication for everything else to work well together.

In website optimization, there's a hidden gem in SEO strategy known as internal linking. It's often underestimated but helps in improving your site's visibility and user experience. Think of it as the glue that holds together the various pieces of content on your website.

When you tactically place internal links, they create a map for search engines, helping them navigate through your website's content maze. As you dive into the world of linking, you'll learn how to blend themes effectively, understand the importance of link authority, and grasp the significance of anchor text.

This guide is here to help you become a master of both internal and backlinking. It provides the tools you need to strengthen your website's authority, navigate the complexities of SEO, and take your online presence to new heights. So, get ready as we explore the world of linking and unlock your website's full potential.

Internal link

Internal link building is a highly underrated practice in SEO. I believe that internal linking is extremely important and should be given significant consideration during the early stages of website planning, specifically when organizing your site's content into silos. To effectively implement internal linking, identify the main themes and sub-themes of your website, along with relevant keywords. This will help you determine where to place links based on commonality. The purpose of linking within your website is to group together similar subjects, allowing search engines to understand the specific topics covered in different sections or pages of your site. By creating a focus and pointing to the main topics, you give clarity to search engines.

Ever wondered how Googlebot navigates from one page to another? Perhaps not, but I'll share a little secret with you as you continue reading. Internal links can be likened to a spider's web behind the scenes of your website. When you link from one page to another within the same domain (sitename.com), search engine bots, often referred to as "spiders," can easily discover and scan all the pages of your site, following a left-to-right, top-to-bottom reading pattern. This process is known as "crawling." Once a page is crawled, it is stored in a vast library, indicating that your website has been "indexed."

When creating internal links, it is best to connect related themes or subjects. However, cross-linking between sub-themes that are not considered main themes can dilute the overall focus. Therefore, it is advisable to only link from non-main theme sub-themes to main themes when necessary. This approach avoids unnecessary linking that may distract search engines from finding what potential site visitors are searching for. However, this doesn't mean you should be stingy with your internal linking efforts. Instead, always prioritize linking between related pages. If the topics of two pages are related, it is highly likely that linking them together is beneficial.

There are numerous benefits to having a generous amount of well-placed internal links. Firstly, it allows visitors to navigate your site more freely, facilitating clicks to additional pages. This provides added value to readers by offering them extra resources to explore or read. Moreover, search engines interpret this as a positive signal, indicating that your website's content is valuable to your target audience, resulting in an SEO boost. Additionally, internal links help search engine crawlers by providing new access points to other areas or pages of your website.

If a particular page possesses strong link authority, it makes sense to transfer or share that power with other pages. In the realm of ranking optimization, there is a concept called "Link Juice," which measures how much authority each link passes to a main or landing page. When a post contains links to other pages, a portion of its PageRank (PR) potential, which ranges from 1 to 100, is transmitted to those linked pages. The higher the page's value, the more link juice it provides when linked or redirected to another page. This ranking weight is distributed among each redirect within your website and other sites on the internet. Therefore, it is advantageous to build links from high-value PR pages that redirect to relevant main pages. It's important to note that as you naturally develop well-structured site pages with notable keywords, backlinks, and valuable content, the PageRank of your main pages will gradually improve over time.

When linking to pages internally or receiving inbound links (backlinks), use hyperlinks or anchor text that matches the main keyword or keyword phrase of the linked page's H1 (heading tag). If an exact match is not possible, using synonyms of the H1 tag as anchor text is a suitable alternative. Avoid using generic phrases like "click here" or "read this," and instead use descriptive anchor text, preferably incorporating a relevant keyword. Employing a variety of anchor text provides more context and aids search engines in understanding the content of the linked page.

Search engines have an insatiable appetite for web links, both internal and inbound. Therefore, ensure that any clickable text containing the appropriate keywords for the linked page, matching its H1 tag. This is important because search engine bots assign weight to these keywords when processing queries.

Websites with blogs and designated landing pages tend to have a higher number of indexed pages compared to those without. This is one reason why I recommend having blogs. Although it may seem daunting and time-consuming initially, there are straightforward ways to tackle this task incrementally, which I will explain later.

Earlier, I discussed how crawling and spiders function to discover and navigate websites and pages. However, have you ever wondered how you can rank your website pages in the top five on Google? Have you come across experts claiming to help you "rank on page one in only 24 hours"? As unbelievable as it may sound, it is indeed possible to achieve significant rankings and attract a flood of site traffic in just a few hours by leveraging Google Console's indexing tool.

Utilize Google Console to expedite the indexing of your website by Google for free. The more blog posts and main landing pages present in the vast library, the higher the chances of your pages appearing in search results for relevant queries. Every time you update or create a post or page, promptly submit the updated page URL through the Google Console tool for indexing. This process takes only seconds and requires minimal effort, allowing up to ten submissions per day.

One of the features of Google Console is to verify that all external and internal links on your site are functioning correctly and do not lead to 404 pages (broken links). Not only does this prevent wasted link juice, but it also ensures a positive user experience, impacting various other metrics. I will provide more details on Google Console in Secret Guide #9, "Track and Analyze Your Efforts."

The great news is that tools like Ahrefs and SEMrush can greatly assist in optimizing internal link building. Ahrefs offers a free service that identifies internal linking opportunities effortlessly.

In addition to your internal link-building efforts, it is important to seek out opportunities to be referenced by reputable websites. These external links that point to your e-commerce business are known as backlinks.

Backlinking

Continuing from the previous discussion on internal link building, it is equally important to focus on acquiring backlinks from reputable websites. Backlinks serve as references to your e-commerce business and solidify your website's authority and visibility in search engine rankings.

When it comes to backlinks, quality matters more than quantity. It's preferable to have a few high-quality backlinks from authoritative websites rather than numerous low-quality links. Search engines consider backlinks as votes of confidence from other websites, indicating that your content is valuable and trustworthy.

To attract valuable backlinks, you need to create compelling and shareable content. This could include informative blog posts, engaging articles, or valuable resources that other website owners or bloggers would find relevant and helpful for their audience. By consistently producing high-quality content, you increase the likelihood of earning backlinks naturally.

Another way to acquire backlinks is through outreach and relationship-building. Identify influential websites or industry experts within your niche and reach out to them, offering to collaborate or provide guest posts. By establishing mutually beneficial relationships, you can secure opportunities for backlinks and expand your online presence.

However, ensure that the backlinks you receive are relevant and contextually appropriate. Search engines assess the relevance of backlinks to determine the credibility and authority they contribute to your website. Therefore, it's important to focus on obtaining backlinks from websites that are topically related to your own. For example, if you operate an online fashion store, backlinks from fashion blogs or industry publications would carry more weight than those from unrelated sources.

It's worth noting that not all backlinks are created equal. The authority and reputation of the linking website play a significant role in the impact of the backlink. Backlinks from highly authoritative and reputable websites have a greater influence and impact on your off-page SEO efforts and website's search engine rankings.

Additionally, the anchor text used in backlinks holds importance. It's beneficial to have anchor text that includes relevant keywords or a variation of them. This helps search engines understand the content of the linked page and further reinforces its relevance and credibility.

Monitoring and analyzing your backlink profile is essential to ensure the quality and effectiveness of your backlinks. Tools like Ahrefs and SEMrush can provide insights into your backlink profile, allowing you to identify any potentially harmful or low-quality backlinks that may negatively impact your SEO efforts. Regularly reviewing and disavowing irrelevant or spammy backlinks is crucial for maintaining a healthy backlink profile.

Acquiring high-quality backlinks from reputable websites is a key aspect of effective SEO. By producing valuable content, engaging in outreach, and cultivating relationships within your industry, you earn relevant and authoritative backlinks that enhance your website's visibility and authority in rankings.

Monitoring and optimizing your backlink profile ensures that you maintain a strong and trustworthy online presence.

Now that you understand linking, you should not have any problems linking page contents throughout your website and inbound sites. This knowledge will prove invaluable as you seek to enhance your e-commerce website for pop-up shop success.

PART IV

Popup Your E-commerce for Success

There are some features I recommend to optimize and Popup Your E-commerce for success. Here is why:

In the tumultuous year of 2020, amid the global pandemic, small businesses operating pop-up shops found these features to be crucial. As a pop-up shop merchant myself, I can attest to their effectiveness, especially during times when outdoor activities were limited. These features facilitated a smoother shopping experience, making it less daunting for customers to visit pop-up shop markets for their essentials. They enabled entrepreneurs to connect with consumers and offer products and services across various neighborhoods in America. However, these features have always been instrumental in driving e-commerce success, pandemic or not. Therefore, including them in your daily operations will prove to be beneficial.

Online Ordering with Event Pickup Option – Create a user-friendly section on your website where customers can place orders online and select pickup at pop-up shop events. This feature should be easy to locate and navigate, allowing customers to browse products, choose pickup dates and times, and complete their purchases. You'll find further information about this topic in Secret Guide #7 under the section titled "Initiate Website Transactions."

Pop-up shop Event Page – Develop a dedicated page on your website that gives detailed information about upcoming pop-up shop events. Include event dates, times, themes, locations, and any other relevant details. Regularly update this page and consider adding a calendar feature for customers to mark their calendars or sign up for event notifications.

Real-Time Event Updates – Ensure your website displays real-time updates about pop-up shop events, including any cancellations or schedule changes. This information should be prominently featured on the event page and communicated to customers through notifications or email newsletters.

Sales Team Showcase – Assign a dedicated section showcasing your sales team on your website. Include their photos, names, bios, and roles within the company. Specify which team members will be present at each pop-up shop location, enabling customers to connect with them during events. Additional details will be discussed later in Secret Guide #8 under the heading "Connections with Teams and Customers."

Interactive Map and Location Details – Include an interactive map on the event page to visually display the pop-up shop location. This map should be easy to navigate and include details such as the address, parking options, public transportation details, and any specific instructions for reaching the venue.

Social Media Inclusion – Have social media buttons and widgets on your website to encourage customers to share and discuss pop-up shop events. Enable social media sharing of event details and updates and display real-time social media feeds related to the events to keep customers engaged and informed.

Having these features on your e-commerce website effectively supports your pop-up shop operation, providing an experience for customers to order online and pick up their purchases at events. Additionally, these will help generate excitement, share information about pop-up events, and enhance customer engagement.

SEO Types

If you're looking to establish a strong foothold among customers in a specific area, local SEO is the way to go. By optimizing your online presence, especially your website, you can effectively target and engage a local audience of loyal patrons. One highly effective strategy to connect with your target audience locally is by creating and optimizing your Google My Business Page.

As promised, below are the other SEO types, including local SEO, that you can employ to help with the success of your e-commerce pop-up shop.

Local SEO – This type of SEO focuses on establishing your business locally and attracting customers within a specific area. By optimizing your website and online content, you effectively reach and engage your target audience in the local community. A key characteristic of local SEO is optimizing your Google My Business Page, which facilitates connecting with local customers.

Technical SEO – To ensure scalability and growth for your e-commerce store, make technical SEO a key player. This involves optimizing your website for factors such as website speed and mobile device compatibility, as well as enhancing web pages with Schema markup. By paying attention to technical SEO, you can improve your site's performance and overall optimization.

Off-Page SEO – While on-page SEO focuses on optimizing your website, off-page SEO involves optimization efforts outside of your website. Social media marketing, guest blogging to attract traffic from relevant sites, and backlink building are examples of off-page SEO techniques. These strategies can help boost your online occurrence and drive more traffic to your pop-up shop and physical storefront.

In this section, I have highlighted examples where these types of SEO are applicable, offering valuable insights that can greatly boost your business. However, before going into practical tasks, check to see if your planning and organization are well executed.

Furthermore, apart from the SEO types and their functioning, here is an additional tip derived from the previous section that can be helpful with the success of your pop-up shop:

Make sure your business is listed in directories that specifically target local search optimization, such as CitySearch, Yelp, EzLocal, and hundreds more. Consistency is key, so verify that the information provided in these directories aligns with the details on your Google My Business Page.

By being keen on and applying these SEO techniques and supplementary strategies, you will establish a strong foundation for success as a pop-up shop entrepreneur. Therefore, commence your journey with thorough planning and organization before starting any hands-on tasks. Best of luck!

While using effective SEO techniques and strategies is essential for the success of your pop-up shop, it can be a time consuming and daunting task to manage on top of the many other responsibilities. Your focus should be on meticulous planning, organization, and practical duties that drive your business forward. This is where content writing services come into play, offering support to reduce your workload. By leveraging professional assistance, you can ensure your online business website remains optimized while freeing up your time and energy to concentrate on core areas of your business. In the next section, I will discuss the benefits of utilizing content writing services and how they can help alleviate the burden of creating compelling and engaging content. So, let's closely look at the topic of content writing services and see how they can improve your productivity and business growth.

Outsourced Writing Services

If you're concerned about managing your business operations and creating consistent website content, outsourcing can be a viable choice. While it may seem overwhelming, understanding the necessary knowledge can protect you from being exploited. As a starting point, I suggest outsourcing content creation to relieve some of your workload, such as blogs, articles, and product pages. Here are four services to ponder:

iWriter – is a platform that connects businesses with freelance writers, offering a streamlined ordering process for a variety of content types, including articles, blog posts, and product descriptions. They provide services like SEO optimization, ghostwriting, and copywriting, and their rating system simplifies writer selection within specific niches, all while keeping costs budget-friendly.

Textbroker – another content creation platform, provides businesses with user-friendly ordering options for articles, blog posts, and product descriptions. They also offer services like SEO optimization, ghostwriting, and copywriting. Utilizing an algorithm, Textbroker matches businesses with writers based on content complexity and subject matter, focusing on cost-effective content solutions.

Contena – Like other platforms, it facilitates connections between businesses and freelance writers. They offer a straightforward ordering process for various content types and services, including SEO optimization, ghostwriting, and copywriting. Contena also employs a rating system to help businesses find specialized writers and strives to deliver affordable content solutions.

HireWriters – Connects businesses with freelance writers and offers a simple ordering process for articles, blog posts, and product descriptions. They provide writing services such as SEO optimization, ghostwriting, and copywriting, using an algorithm to match businesses with appropriate writers based on content complexity and subject matter. HireWriters aims to provide cost-effective solutions for obtaining high-quality content.

AI Content Generators

Technology is advancing fast, and one of the exciting developments is artificial intelligence. One cool example of this is ChatGPT, which is a smart computer program made by a company called OpenAI. It's been trained to understand and write in a way that's almost like how people talk.

This makes ChatGPT useful for having conversations, answering questions, and doing lots of different tasks like translating languages, summarizing text, and even creating stories and poems.

In this section, we'll look at how AI content generators like ChatGPT work and why fine-tuning them is important for making them better at specific jobs. With this AI-powered content creation, it's getting harder to tell if a human or a machine is doing the creating.

ChatGPT – This is an AI-powered language model developed by OpenAI. It is based on the transformer architecture and is trained on a large corpus of text data from the internet. The model has been fine-tuned to generate human-like text, making it capable of responding to questions and having conversations with users.

ChatGPT can be used for a variety of purposes, including language translation, text summarization, and question-answering. It can also be used to generate creative writing, such as fiction or poetry, or to chat with users in a more conversational setting.

World Tune – Fine-tuning, also known as transfer learning, is a process in which a pre-trained machine learning model is further trained on a smaller dataset specific to a particular task. The idea behind fine-tuning is that the model has already learned many general-purpose features from the large-scale pre-training, so it can adapt more quickly to the new task with less data.

When it comes to language models like ChatGPT, fine-tuning helps to enhance their performance for specific tasks such as answering questions, generating creative writing, or translating text.

Putting Insights into Action

Now that you have gained loads of information from this Secret Guide, it's time to apply that knowledge to your e-commerce business. Whether you already have a website or are starting from scratch, it's important to focus on optimizing your online business website as best as you can. Start by evaluating the current ranking of your website's pages using tools like Ahrefs or other free and paid services. These tools will help you identify which pages are performing well and which ones need improvement, allowing you to refine your strategies appropriately.

Additionally, assess each page and affiliated websites, aiming to address weaknesses and uncover opportunities to enhance the content, design, and overall user experience. By following and using my guidelines, you can easily align your brand's message and theme. Ensure that all aspects of your company, including your website and other platforms, consistently reflect your brand's central purpose and value proposition.

SEO AND CENTRAL PURPOSE WORKSHEET
– Prepare for Dream Customers.

1. What is your business's core market desire? (Choose from Wealth, Health, or Relationships)

_____

_____

_____

_____

_____

2. What submarket(s) and niche(s) does your business fall under within your chosen core market? *Submarket (E.g., Online Business Tools, Nutrition, Dating), Niche(s) (E.g., Online Marketplace, Paleo diet, how to make a good first impression)*

_____

_____

_____

_____

_____

3. Describe your company's central purpose in one concise sentence. How does your business add value to your target audience within your core market and submarket(s)?

_____

_____

_____

_____

_____

4. Use the information provided to identify a main theme and sub themes for your e-commerce website.

Main Theme: _____

Sub Themes: _____

1. _____
2. _____
3. _____

Craft a H1 main heading and H2 subheading for the homepage of your e-commerce website.

H1 Main Heading: _____
H2 Subheading: _____

KEYWORD MANAGEMENT WORKSHEET –
Follow the Example.

Keyword	Search Volume	Keyword Difficulty	CPC (Cost Per Click)	Current Ranking	SERP Feature	Intent (Informational, Navigational, Transactional)	Notes
Targeted Keyword	10,000	50	$1.10	15	Image Pack	Informational	Competitor X, ranks #3

Table Columns Explained:

Keyword: The specific search term you're targeting.
Search Volume: The average monthly search volume for the keyword.

Keyword Difficulty: A metric (usually from 0 to 100) indicating how hard it is to rank for this keyword.

CPC (Cost Per Click): The average cost per click if you were to use PPC advertising for this keyword.

Current Ranking: Your website's current position in search engine results for this keyword.

SERP Features: Special features in search engine results (like featured snippets, image packs, FAQ, reviews) that could affect visibility.

Intent: The searcher's intended action (informational, navigational, transactional) can help tailor content to match.

Notes: Any additional observations or strategies for   improvement.

This table should be regularly updated with fresh data and reviewed to adjust strategies as needed. Tools like Google Analytics, SEMrush, Ahrefs, or Moz can provide the necessary metrics to fill in this table. Use the example to create your own table or download a free copy at:

www.popupyourecommerce.com/manage-keywords

SECRET GUIDE #3

Align Brand Message and Theme

Make All Medium Similarly Reflects Brands Purpose and Value Preposition.

In this Secret Guide, I will primarily discuss the importance of consistency of brand presentation online and offline. The starting point is making your value proposition, theme, and headlines consistent across all marketing channels. By aligning your brand message and theme, you create a cohesive identity that reflects your brand's purpose, allowing you to captivate your audience. I will also share the power of maintaining a unified presence in various media outlets, helping your company to establish a strong and recognizable brand where e-commerce and pop-up shops coexist.

PART I

Brand Message Familiarization

The following important milestone is to send signals to your core audience using proper, consistent, or aligned branding. Remember, the target audience or core market refers to the intended patrons who desire your products or services. These are the people who will easily notice the message displayed in all marketing media. This instant connection usually happens since it speaks to the frustration they have or the problem they are trying to solve. These communicative materials should not only connect but consistently do so. It should similarly be presented everywhere your business exists. Consistent and similar means using the same color scheme, theme, message, logo, slogan, and taglines. The overall brand design must equally be represented at your pop-up shop, physical storefront, social media business pages, online marketplaces, and e-commerce website. Everyone should know it's your company, no matter where you operate physically or digitally online. This does not only help with building a robust brand identity, but it also prevents your followers and supporters from mistakenly bypassing you.

Your company's taglines, photos, and headlines must be so impactful that your dream clients should have no doubt you can help solve their needs. Additionally, the list in the previous sentence must also give off the same vibes wherever they are shown. Furthermore, they must be presented in a way that will represent the overall company's core market, submarket, and niche discussed in the previous secret. For example, if your business is proposing healthy organic skin care soaps for overall body healing, the taglines, photos, and headlines must reflect that on all communication technologies at your pop-up shop, i.e., banners.

As a rule of thumb, reference your e-commerce website homepage and landing pages for design ideas to be included on banners, customized tents, brochures, or any other advertising exhibits you will use at venues. For your regulars, they will know it is you immediately, no matter where you operate your business.

Explicitly cater advertisement and branding to a specific audience or group of people. Please do not attempt to gain all people as loyal patrons; instead, aim to connect with everyone. No company is established to serve all people. In other words, it is not necessary or realistic for a company to try to attract every single person as a devoted customer. Instead, focus on building connections and engaging with as many people as possible. Out of those connections, a few will become loyal, and that's all you need to build and grow strong.

Your business will serve your core market well with the right message. Although this is true, others will buy from you at pop-up venues regardless of whether they are your targeted group, which I will explain further in the next section.

Even though you will receive and connect with random supporters at your booth, organic e-commerce website visitors, on the other hand, most often do not buy unless your product or service solves their needs, except for pop-up shop customers who are directed to your site by you from venues. Natural website visitors happen regularly, with organic traffic coming to your site since people are searching for specific information or products on search engines. Also, when you are sharing your site pages on social media, it's best to share with specific groups that you think may want what you sell. This is referred to as identifying your "Dream 100" customers, as Russel Brunson explained in his "Traffic Secrets" book. Dream 100 is essentially finding where your audience congregates online, for example, social media groups, and attempting to market to those folks in several locations.

Clearly targeting and marketing to a group with the right and consistent message may be the most challenging yet rewarding journey for any business. Therefore, you must identify and connect well with your potential dream customers when you meet them online and offline.

Maximizing Brand Messaging

Online businesses participating in pop-up shops connect with customers in a tangible and immersive way. At this point, that's no longer a secret. But avoid wasting resources and time on misleading and irrelevant brand information. While not every customer may be seeking a life-changing experience, some individuals may still make impulsive and supportive purchases. They may be driven by the desire to support small and micro-size businesses in their local communities, or they may be in search of specialty gift products or specific services. In these cases, still effectively deliver your brand message because these customers may have networks to potential die-hard fans who genuinely need what you have.

Diverse Customer Motivations

It is important to acknowledge that customer motivations are diverse and go beyond immediate, life-altering advantages. People are motivated by different things, including a strong sense of community and a desire to actively contribute to their respective neighborhoods. Additionally, there are those who seek unique experiences tailored to their specific needs. It's worth noting that some pop-up shoppers are often willing to advocate for your business to others who would genuinely find value in what you trade for money. Leveraging word-of-mouth recommendations can work wonders in driving brand growth and customer acquisition.

Word-of-Mouth Endorsements

Word-of-mouth recommendations are a major part of the growth and success of any business. When customers have positive experiences with a brand, they are more likely to share their satisfaction with their personal networks, generating word-of-mouth referrals. These endorsements hold weight and credibility, often surpassing the impact of traditional advertising. By delivering a clear and compelling message, you increase the likelihood of positive word-of-mouth spreading, thus attracting a wider audience of potential clientele. Learn more in Secret Guide #4, the section titled "The Power of Word-of-Mouth."

Tips for Branding

Achieving success in branding depends on finding the right balance between being honest, connecting emotionally, being clear, and staying consistent. By making transparency a priority in how they communicate, creating content that appeals to emotions, and explaining clear solutions to problems, brands can genuinely connect with the people they want to reach.

Honesty and Transparency – Avoid misleading brand messaging that overpromises or misrepresents. Instead, focus on transparent communication that accurately reflects your products and services and how it can address customers' needs and desires.

Emotionally Engaging Content – Craft messages that evoke emotions and forge a genuine bond with customers. Appeal to their aspirations, values, or desires, creating a lasting impact.

Clear Problem-Solution Communication – Clearly articulate how your brand solves a problem or fulfills a particular need that fits in one of the core market desires of Health, Wealth, or Relationships. Use language that is relatable, concise, and easy to understand, ensuring that customers immediately grasp the benefits of engaging with your pop-up shop.

Consistency Across Channels – Maintain consistency in your messaging across all online and offline channels, including your website, social media, and pop-up shop events. This coherence reinforces brand identity and enhances customer recognition and recollection.

Engagement and Relationship Building – Actively engage with customers during pop-up shop events, fostering meaningful interactions and building relationships. Personalized experiences and exceptional customer service can leave a lasting impression and encourage word-of-mouth referrals, online reviews, and testimonials. Refer to the next secret guide for detailed information on how to build customer engagement.

Participating in pop-up shops presents an exciting engagement with customers. By avoiding misleading branding and effectively delivering your message, you are likely to capture the attention and interest of diverse groups of people. Even those who may not be seeking a life-changing experience from you.

To reiterate, people supporting small businesses for specialty gift purchases and community-driven motivations are valid reasons for them to engage with your company. Leveraging word-of-mouth recommendations can further amplify your reach and attract potential die-hard fans who genuinely need and benefit from your products or services.

By employing these strategies for effective branding and cultivating positive customer experiences, your e-commerce business will thrive in the pop-up shop arena.

Broadcasting and Engagement

Pop-up shops have become increasingly popular in the retail industry as a creative way to engage with customers and showcase brand culture. Beyond their immediate benefits, pop-ups offer a chance to find a new fan base and expand reach through event broadcasting. This section will highlight the potential of pop-up shops for brand broadcasting and provide information on aligning branding on social media.

Identifying Potential Loyal Fans

The process of identifying potential loyal fans to visit your participating venues involves reaching out to individuals who may have a genuine interest in your company. A pop-up shop is intended to serve as a temporary physical space where you can meet up with your audience face-to-face on a more personal level, and it allows ways to attract and engage potential fans.

To successfully reach out to your dream fanbase, it's best to employ various promotional campaigns across multiple channels.

As you know by now, one avenue is through your social media, where you can regularly post updates and announcements about your upcoming events. By consistently sharing enticing content and creating a buzz around your mobile shops, you pique the curiosity of your followers and potentially convert them into dedicated supporters.

In addition to social media, extend your reach by using online communities and groups that affiliate with your brand and target demographic. With active involvement in these communities and sharing information about your pop-up events, you tap into a highly engaged audience who may already have an interest in what your company brings to the marketplace. Engaging with these groups through thoughtful discussions and input can further grow your brand's reputation.

Another effective way is to collaborate with relevant podcasts and participate in interviews or discussions that focus on topics related to your industry. This showcases your expertise and generates awareness about your pop-up events to a much wider audience. By selecting podcasts that support your company's values and target market, you further increase the likelihood of appealing to prospects who are interested in doing business with you.

Furthermore, having blog posts on your website serves as an informative and engaging place to also promote your shop's venues. By creating compelling and detailed articles that highlight your pop-up events, you offer various topics that garner interest among your website visitors. These blog posts can serve as a resource for people who are actively seeking information about topics related to your niche, ultimately leading them to consider visiting your shop locations to get firsthand experience.

To gauge the level of interest among your audience and identify potential fans, track and analyze engagement metrics.

Monitoring website visits, event registrations, and social media interactions captures the behavior of individuals who are actively engaging with your company and expressing interest. Once you have pinpointed these individuals, prioritize them as likely supporters and tailor your marketing efforts toward converting them into loyal customers.

Consistency in Social Broadcasting

To successfully represent your brand, consistent social broadcasting should reflect its identity. Once again, this includes elements such as colors, photos, designs, and verbiage that are easily recognizable and strongly convey the intended message. While initial postings may not always generate significant engagement, maintaining uniqueness and building engagement over time, you might attract a few inquisitive persons. Through targeting the right audience, like the "Dream 100," and delivering a consistent message, it creates long-term steady growth and build loyalty on social media.

Aligning Social Media

Below, I present a concise reference list outlining the steps to ensure a consistent alignment of messaging and themes across various social media. Please follow these guidelines:

Define the brand message – Begin by clearly defining the mission, values, and key messages that capture your brand's essence. This clarity will lay the foundation for consistency amongst all social channels.

Develop a social media style guide – Create a comprehensive style guide that outlines the desired tone, voice, and language to be used on each social media. This guide will serve as a reference for all social media interactions, ensuring a cohesive brand representation.

Consistent visuals – Use consistent visual branding elements such as logos, color schemes, and imagery across all social media. This visual coherence helps create a unified and recognizable brand image.

Establish a content calendar – Plan and organize a content calendar that defines the type of content to be shared on each platform and the frequency of posts. This ensures a steady flow of engaging content while maintaining the brand's overall messaging.

Train employees – Provide training to employees that's responsible for representing the company on social media. This training must focus on team members understanding the brand's messaging, voice, and guidelines to maintain consistency in interactions.

Monitor and adjust – Continuously monitor social media activity, engagement metrics, and audience feedback. Regularly evaluate and adjust the messaging as necessary to ensure alignment across all channels and resonate with your audience.

Leveraging pop-up shops for effective brand broadcasting offers numerous benefits, including identifying potential loyal fans and expanding reach. By aligning brand messages to various social media networks, you can establish a dependable, compelling, and relevant brand image. Following the outlined steps, from defining the message to monitoring and adjusting social media activities, enables engagement, loyalty, and long-term growth.

Event Marketing Tools

Pop-up shops are a popular marketing plan for businesses to generate awareness, engage with customers, and increase revenue. When executed, it delivers an experience that leaves a lasting impression on individuals you hope to reach. This section discussion will focus on the elements of pop-up shop marketing and advertising, namely banners, tents (canopies), flags, brochures, and business cards, and how they contribute to conveying consistent and clear brand communication.

Banners (Communication Technology)

Banners serve as eye-catching displays that instantly draw attention to your shop. An elaborately designed banner with vibrant colors, bold typography, and the incorporation of the brand logo creates a strong visual impact. Consistency in brand elements, such as using your company's color palette and fonts, ensures that the banner ties in with its overall identity. The banner should clearly communicate the purpose of the pop-up shop business, highlighting any special promotions and products or services to entice shoppers.

Tents (Canopies)

Tents or canopies, if used, play a vital role in establishing a physical presence for your shop. These structures provide shelter, define the space, and contribute to the overall ambiance. A well-designed tent should prominently feature your company's logo, colors, and key messaging to create an organized and engaging atmosphere. The placement of the tent, whether in a high foot-traffic vacant storefront area or at a sponsored event, can enhance visibility and attract the people your company was made to serve.

Flags

Flags extend your brand's reach beyond the pop-up shop's immediate vicinity. Placing branded flags strategically around the shop area, especially in high-traffic locations, can grab the attention of passersby. Just like banners and tents, flags should showcase consistent brand elements to ensure instant recognition. Consider using flags to highlight key messages or to guide visitors toward specific areas of interest within the pop-up shop.

Brochures

Brochures serve as informative marketing materials that provide detailed information about your company, products, and services. These printed materials should be visually appealing, with a clear hierarchy of information and captivating imagery. To maintain brand consistency, brochures should feature the same color scheme, fonts, and imagery as other pop-up shop marketing materials. Including a call-to-action, QR code scanner, and contact details encourages guests to engage further with your brand online after their pop-up shop visit.

Business Cards

Business cards are essential for networking and creating awareness. These small yet powerful marketing tools should feature your brand logo, QR code scanners, contact information, and a concise tagline that communicates your brand's essence. Design the business cards in line with the pop-up shop's overall aesthetic, ensuring consistency in colors, fonts, and imagery. Encourage recipients to re-visit your shop by offering exclusive promotions or discounts.

Branded Uniforms

Branded uniforms worn by your team or representatives at the pop-up shops reinforce identity and create a professional image. These uniforms should prominently display the logo, colors, and key messaging to match the overall distinctiveness.

Customized Printed QR Codes

Having customized printed QR codes onto the uniforms offers an interactive and engaging experience for customers. These codes can be designed to incorporate your brand logo or other relevant visuals, making them visually appealing. By scanning the QR code using their smartphones, customers gain instant access to specific information, promotions, testimonials, or even exclusive discounts online. This mix of technology with uniforms enhances engagement and encourages shoppers to explore your company further than an offline experience.

Brand Information Display

In addition to the QR codes, displaying relevant information on the uniforms further reinforces your key messages. This can include brand statement, tagline, or unique selling points. By showcasing this info on the uniforms, you communicate your company's core purpose and value to customers, for a deeper connection and understanding.

By including branded uniforms with customized printed QR codes and prominently displayed information, it establishes a cohesive and professional image and creates an interactive and informative experience. This integration blends offline and online interactions, allowing customers to explore your company beyond the physical confines of a pop-up shop.

Pop-up shop marketing relies on various elements, including banners, tents (canopies), flags, brochures, and business cards, to convey a clear message. These tools capture attention, create an inviting space, enhance visibility, inform customers, and establish personal and digital influences. By maintaining consistency in design elements and combining key brand messages, it maximizes exposure, engages with various types of shoppers, and ultimately drive sales through pop-up shop marketing.

PART II

E-Commerce Website Marketing

Online shopping is changing, where many businesses are vying for the attention of digital customers, effective marketing is the key to success. Think of your e-commerce website as your digital store, and the messages you use across your online presence as the tools that can make a real difference. Whether it's the attractive homepage, the engaging about page, the informative blog posts, or the lively interactions on your social media, every part plays a role in shaping your brand.

To create an engaging website, it's important to know who your website visitors are and what they expect from you. Identify the people who are interested in your products or services. Find out things like their age, interests, and how they behave as customers. Understanding their needs, wants, and any problems they have will help you create a website that speaks to them.

If you haven't already, it's important to define what your brand stands for and what it wants to achieve. This means clearly stating the values that guide your business and the big mission it's working toward. Make the values and mission align with what your target audience cares about and believes in. Your online store should reflect these principles.

In the following section, I will explain how to create effective marketing messages for different parts of your website. My aim is to make sure that your brand's voice connects strongly with your main audience, both online and offline. So, stay tuned and uncover the secrets of successful e-commerce website marketing, helping you establish a memorable online company.

Home Page

The home page of an e-commerce website serves as the first impression and the gateway to your online branding. It needs to be engaging, visually pleasing, and immediately convey the value your company delivers. The marketing message should focus on capturing the attention of visitors and encouraging them to explore further. Key elements to include are:

Clear Brand Identity – The home page should prominently display the logo, tagline, and unique selling proposition (USP). This helps in building recognition and communicating the core values.

Compelling Headline – A catchy headline that reverberates with the target audience can grab attention and generate interest. It should highlight the key benefits and solutions your business addresses.

Featured Products or Services – Show popular products/services on the home page is designed to entice visitors and encourage them to go beyond the homepage. Highlight key features, promotions, or discounts to create a sense of urgency.

Call-to-Action (CTA) – Encourage visitors to act by using prominent and persuasive CTAs. For example, "Shop Now," "Learn More," or "Subscribe" buttons and hyperlinks can guide users to desired actions.

Testimonials or Reviews – Including customer testimonials or reviews on the home page can instill trust and credibility in your brand. Displaying positive feedback and ratings helps build confidence in potential customers.

About Page

The about page for the most part share company story, mission, and values. It is a chance to establish an emotional connection with site visitors and build trust. The marketing message for the about page should focus on:

Brand Story – Communicate the origin of the brand, its journey, and the passion that drives it. Highlight any unique aspects or values that differentiate you from your competitors.

Mission and Vision – Clearly state the brand's purpose, what it aims to achieve, and how it contributes to the lives of customers or society as a whole. Emphasize the positive impact your company strives to make.

Team and Expertise – Introduce the key members of your team, their qualifications, and expertise. This adds a personal touch and showcases the company's dedication to quality and expertise.

Customer Focus – Highlight the brand's commitment to customer satisfaction, whether through excellent service, personalized experiences, or going the extra mile. Let customers know they are valued.

Blogs

Blogs fulfill a key function in content marketing and building brand recognition. They provide education, entertainment, and engage website visitors. The marketing message for blog pages should:

Address Customer Pain Points – Find common challenges or questions faced by the target audience and offer valuable solutions through the blog posts. Show that your company understands their needs.

Showcase Expertise – Position your company as a thought leader in its industry by providing well-researched, informative, thought provoking, and insightful content and topics related to the problem your company addresses. This helps to build credibility.

Engage with Stories – Use storytelling techniques to captivate readers and make the content relatable. Share success stories, case studies, or user-generated content to demonstrate real-world benefits.

Encourage Interaction – Include social sharing buttons, comments sections, and calls-to-action to encourage readers to engage, share, and see other parts of the website with internal linking.

Social Media Business Pages

Social media direct means of connecting with people is helpful with brand building. Therefore, the marketing messages for your social media business pages should be:

Consistency and Coherence – Ensure that your company identity, messaging, and visual elements are consistent at all social media network. This strengthens brand recognition and creates an interconnected experience.

Engaging Content – Share a variety of content types, including product updates, behind-the-scenes glimpses, customer stories, and relevant industry news. Strive for a balance between educational, promotional, and entertaining content.

Community Building – Encourage followers to interact with your company by running contests, hosting live events, or soliciting user-generated content. This adopts a sense of community and loyalty.

Timely and Responsive – Respond to comments, messages, and mentions in a timely manner. Show that your company values its followers and is actively engaged in conversations.

Influencer Partnerships – Collaborate with influencers or industry experts to expand reach, gain credibility, and tap into their followers. This helps in building awareness and attracting new customers.

Developing marketing messages that will work well for e-commerce websites requires good planning. Focusing on things, such as brand identity, value proposition, customer engagement, and building trust, creates compelling messages that echo to your core audience.

Creating a Unified Brand Identity

As you may realize by now, aim to a have consistent message, look, and feel everywhere your people see your company, whether online or in a physical manner. This helps to become more recognizable and makes people feel a stronger connection to it.

To make this work put it in writing first. Therefore, refer to the worksheet for your drafted brand message you should have already completed. Review it and ensure it correctly states your company's values, mission, and what makes it special compared to other brands. Remember your brand's theme is how it looks visually—like the logo, colors, fonts, and pictures you use. These things together create your company's unique style.

Once you have a clear message and theme, see to it that they're the same everywhere people find your company. Here are some additional pointers to help with that:

Keep the Same Look – Use the same logo, colors, and fonts on your website, social media, products, and physical stores. This helps people recognize you quickly.

Use the Same Writing Style – Decide if your brand echoes formal, friendly, or funny, and stick with that style in everything you write, like on your website, in emails, and on social media. This makes everything feel consistent.

Share Your Brand's Story – Craft a story that represents what your brand stands for. Include this story in all your messages to make the brand more appealing and relatable. Storytelling is an absolute must. Use storytelling techniques to mix important messages into interesting stories that grab people's attention. Use clear language, compelling visuals, and relatable stories to convey your values and mission. By creating narratives that connect with your audience's experiences, problems, and dreams, you will have a memorable and powerful message.

Make Things Easy for Customers – Verify your website and other online places are easy to use and navigate. This makes people want to come back.

Use All Your Marketing Channels Together – If your company is online and offline, use all the different ways you connect with customers to share the same message. Whether people find you on your website, social media, in a store, or at an event, they should get the same feeling about your brand.

Learn from Feedback – Pay close attention to what people say about your company online. This can help you find areas where you are not consistent or need improvement. Then, use this feedback to potentially make improvements.

In a nutshell, making certain your business has a clear message and looks the same everywhere is important. When your company looks and sounds the same in all the places, it becomes more memorable.

Brand Consistency Importance

Obviously, consistency is a big deal in a company's marketing effort. It's like having a reliable and predictable personality. When your business behaves the same way with customers, employees, and other important people like stakeholders, it shows that it's serious about its values, reliability, and being good at what it does. In this part, I'll explain further why this is so important, especially when it comes to the culture of your brand.

Being consistent helps keep a company's brand culture steady. When a business sticks to its core values, mission, and vision, it creates stability and reliability for everyone involved, both inside and outside the company. Employees who believe in brand values and understand what the company is all about can work together toward common goals. This applies to outside folks, too, like investors and business partners, who want to know they can count on the company. A stable brand culture makes the company perceived to be reliable and trustworthy, which builds confidence and attracts chances for growth and teamwork.

Creating a strong and consistent message, both online and offline, helps with a successful brand. By following the steps outlined in this guide, your business can effectively convey its values, mission, and unique selling points. It's essential to keep refining your message based on user feedback and analytics so that your website and other communication channels convey information that builds lasting connections. This includes engaging with pop-up shop visitors who are browsing your booth and checking out your website.

BRAND MESSAGE & THEME WORKSHEET –
Create a Cohesive Identity.

1. How can referencing your e-commerce website help maintain consistency in various advertising exhibits?

_____

_____

_____

_____

_____

2. What information should be displayed on uniforms to reinforce key messages?

_____

_____

_____

_____

_____

SECRET GUIDE #4
Build Customer En-gagement

Engage with Each Person on the Other Side of your Booth.

PART I

Supercharge your E-commerce Business

The purpose of building customer engagement is for the relationship, awareness, and the brand loyalty it promotes. Making engagement a big part of your overall pop-up strategy is a transformational one. This may be the secret sauce to why companies blow up overnight, and we look in awe. Why? That blow-up was not overnight. After all, their customer engagement strategies, over time, delivered tremendous results. Have you ever wondered why digital arenas make engagement a measuring clue to gauge a company's performance?

Obviously, without it, the needle doesn't move. Things will remain the same. With an engaging online business, you influence visitors to move and act with the value you give. The value may include interactive blog posts, videos, new product offerings, beautifully displayed photos, and nicely blended colors.

The same applies to your pop-up booth operations. Create well-laid-out table schematics that fit the event traffic flow with an inviting feel for shoppers to navigate. Formulate a color arrangement that's vibrant and attractive. Furthermore, banners and scannable QR materials should be included, along with a well-written value statement. Customers need to be engaged and receive full experience. Whenever you have pop-up guests, all action is ideal. Treat it like a party, celebrating how you can change someone's life for the better with your product(s) or service(s).

For example, while at your pop-up, encourage shoppers and onlookers to give online reviews or conduct surveys after they have scanned your QR code. The experience should evoke the excitement of paparazzi, with customers taking and sharing images of your display and website address. They should feel inspired to spread the word to friends, family, and groups through social media and text messages.

Also, remember to pay close attention to what customers are saying and discussing. Likewise, watch how they act and their expressions when you help them. To confirm that you have done a good job, ask a question like, 'Did I help you satisfactorily today? This enables you to provide good service and receive quick feedback. If they had a bad experience, you could address the issue before they decide to negatively engage with your brand online.

These engagement activities, wherever they may be online or offline, help you make decisions as your organization grows. Therefore, as you "*Popup Your E-commerce,*" you will generate more revenue just simply by engaging people on the other side of the booth.

QR Code Marketing for Engagement

Here, you will learn how to use QR codes to enhance the popup shop experience and generate online buzz. In this readthrough, I will outline the steps to create informational QR codes, encourage customers to scan them, and share your content. By following these simple yet effective steps, your company's web presence can skyrocket, potentially leading to viral exposure and increased interest.

Step 1: Create Captivating QR Codes – To begin, design QR codes that direct users to webpages showcasing your products or services. Customize the codes to support your specific goals; they could lead to Google for reviews, your social media account for likes and follows, or even special landing pages for product rollouts and promotions. These scannable codes must be accessible, visually appealing, informative, and easy to navigate at your pop-up booth display, ensuring an easy user experience.

Step 2: Printing QR Codes for Maximum Visibility – To make it simple, use tools like Microsoft Word to download and print QR codes. I recommend that you add these codes to your promotional materials like flyers, posters, T-shirts with your brand logo, or business cards. This way, they'll grab people's attention and be easy for your pop-up shop guests to access. You can also place the codes on your booth's table using risers or even on your uniform, just like I've discussed before. The goal is to make it super convenient for customers to scan them.

Step 3: Scanning QR Codes with Smartphones – Customers with their modern devices and smartphones can directly use their built-in QR code readers to scan codes with ease. For those without this feature, a free QR code reader app download will suffice, or have them use their phone cameras. Please see to it that the scanning process is smooth to encourage engagement.

Step 4: Directing Customers to Engaging Webpages – Once a customer scans the code, they are redirected to your designated webpage or any other business pages online, for example, Etsy marketplace. However, making your e-commerce website the primary destination can be a smart choice, as it allows customers to fully engage with your business online.

Step 5: Encouraging Social Media Sharing – Present content on your website that aligns with the enticing presentation of your pop-up shop. With delivering value and brand experience, customers are more likely to share site links to their social media audience.

Therefore, include share buttons on webpages to facilitate easy sharing or allow them to copy and paste the link directly.

Step 6: Going Viral and Expanding Your Reach – As the shared links circulate among website visitors or customer's friends and followers, the potential for virality increases. Quality content and a compelling offer can encourage further sharing, resulting in a cascade snowball effect of online exposure.

By having QR codes and visible URLs in the pop-up shop experience, you continue to bridge the gap between offline and online marketing. These codes, when combined with engaging web pages and shareable content, appeal to customers and prospects, encouraging them to spread the word about your business. As your website traffic and leads grow, you'll witness the real impact of your accessible QR codes and their ability to help boost visibility, leading to sales and business growth.

Social Media Engagement

Let's talk more about using social media to promote your pop-up shop. It's important to realize how much of a difference it can make for your brand's visibility and interaction. Here's what you can do to make the most of it.

Being Present on Multiple Platforms – Take advantage of your occurrence on various social media like Facebook, Instagram, Twitter, TikTok, and Pinterest. If you're not on any of these yet, it's never too late to start with at least one. Each social media network caters to different groups of people with varying interests, allowing connection with a broader audience.

Consistent Branding – Maintain a consistent brand image across all your social media profiles. This means using the same logo, color scheme, and messaging tone. As you learned earlier, consistency helps build brand familiarity and trust.

Creating Engaging Content – Create and share content that keeps your audience engaged. This can include behind-the-scenes glimpses of your pop-up shop setup, testimonials, product demonstrations, or informative posts related to your industry. Keep your people engaged by sharing a mix of photos, videos, and written information.

Encouraging User-Generated Content (UGC) – Don't forget to always tell your customers to share their experiences at your pop-up shop venues on social media while using specified hashtags that you will give them. Share and celebrate this user-generated content on your own profiles to build a sense of community. UGC is a powerful form of social proof.

Using Interactive Features – Take advantage of the interactive features provided by social media, such as polls, quizzes, stories, and live streaming. These features allow real-time engagement and feedback from your audience.

QR Codes – As mentioned earlier, strategically incorporate QR codes into your social media strategy. When customers scan these QR codes, they should be directed to your social space or website. This provides measurable results for your digital marketing efforts.

Analytics and Insights – Regularly analyze the performance of your social campaigns using built-in analytics tools or third-party software. Pay attention to metrics like engagement rates, click-through rates, and conversion rates. Learn more about these tools in Secret Guide #9 and use them to refine your strategy for better results.

Consider Paid Advertising – Consider investing in paid advertising to reach a larger and more targeted audience. Social media offers advanced targeting options, allowing you to reach people based on demographics, interests, and behaviors.

Building a Community – Create a sense of belonging by actively engaging with your followers during and after your pop-up events have ended. Respond to comments and messages promptly and participate in relevant conversations within your niche. Building a strong online community can lead to loyal customers who advocate on your behalf.

Collaborate and Use Influencer Marketing – Partner with local influencers or micro-influencers who share your company's values. Their endorsement can introduce your pop-up shop to a new and engaged audience.

Social media engagement is a requisite act for promoting your shop. By following these best practices, you can generate excitement, increase awareness, and ultimately drive more business to your booth and e-commerce website.

The Power of Word-of-Mouth

Picture this scenario: You are at a vibrant pop-up event showcasing your business to a diverse group of people. Among the crowd, a person stands out as they show genuine interest. They engage with your sales members, asking questions, exploring your products, and eventually making a purchase. Little do you know; this initial transaction marks the beginning of a powerful marketing phenomenon – Customer Engagement and Advocacy (CEAA).

When a customer engages with your company, it goes beyond just making a purchase. They form a connection with your business, understand your values, and witness firsthand quality. This emotional bonding and satisfaction with their purchase often lead to them becoming advocates.

The act of advocacy entails more than mere satisfaction; it involves enthusiastically sharing their positive experience with others. Whether it be through dialogs with friends, family members, colleagues, or with social media strangers, these advocates act as passionate ambassadors. They speak highly of your business, making recommendations with genuine praise and appreciation for the value they received.

It's no secret that word-of-mouth marketing is a prevailing force, and customer advocacy serves as its most potent catalyst. The shared scanned link, exchanged between an advocate and someone they know, serves as a direct pathway to your company across the web. It lures the interest of potential customers, drawing them to your virtual storefront.

Upon visiting your online shop, these intrigued prospects can see more of your offerings. They can read reviews and testimonials from other satisfied customers, validating the positive feedback they received from the advocate. This validation strengthens the credibility and trustworthiness of your brand in the eyes of these new prospects.

Furthermore, the transition from a one-time event purchase to a frequent online shopper becomes more compelling due to the engaging experience they had at an event. The initial face-to-face contact creates a foundation of trust, and the convenience of online shopping becomes an attractive option when they are unable to meet you and your team in person.

This is where what I call the 360-degree marketing tactic comes into play. Such a maneuver ensures that every touchpoint and interaction with your brand is well-built to create a consistent and positive customer experience. From the event itself, where customers first encounter your startup pop-up storefront, then to your e-commerce website, where they make repeat purchases online, or to your brick-and-mortar storefront, where they visit and shop. Every step is carefully arranged to delight and engage.

The 360-degree marketing I speak of also helps with various marketing tools, both online and offline, to establish a brand occurrence. From social media marketing, email campaigns, and content creation to personalized customer support, loyalty programs, and user-generated content, every part of your marketing strategy works in congruence to reinforce Customer Engagement and Advocacy.

The power of CEAA lies in the genuine connection formed between your company and customers. When individuals become advocates, they willingly spread the word, directing others to your online shop.

By adopting a 360-degree marketing campaign, which I will explain further in detail later, you create an all-in-one experience that solidifies customer loyalty and continually attracts new prospects, even in the absence of face-to-face interactions. Embrace the power of CEAA and watch your company thrive through the enthusiasm of your very satisfied patrons.

Align Engagement

In the marketplace, shoppers are expecting consistently aligned experiences across multiple channels. Therefore, while this secret is focused on engaging your audience at your pop-up shops, followed by across the world wide web, please review the prior secret to ensure all your channels similarly or uniformly represent your brand. Also, as you evolve or pivot any parts of your business, verify your websites, social media, phone apps, storefront, and pop-up shops are updated to maintain a uniform representation.

It needs to be this way so that when people are engaging with you, it is easier for them to keep focused and participate, wherever you may be, while you take them on a journey, offline to online or vice versa, and not divert. Remember, customers are visiting you in many places to engage. They need to know they are backing a company that they intuitively desire to support. If they are unsure, they will not engage. These may include but are not limited to taking photos of your booth, scanning a QR code, signing up to your email list, making a purchase, reading your blog, giving a review, a follow or like on social media, or simply doing whatever you want them to do.

Doing these things builds client-to-business relationships, trust, and good communication. Hence, your company creates an omnichannel customer engagement that delivers dependable service across all touchpoints and channels.

Omnichannel Engagement

The term omnichannel basically means having an active 360-degree marketing strategy for your ongoing pop-up shop operation. This omnichannel or 360-degree marketing must be done throughout the lifecycle of your business. This is a way to operate online with the support of pop-up shops and/or a physical brick-and-mortar storefront. It is an impressive way to join platforms together to deliver a complete experience that makes ongoing engagement possible. The purpose of this, while you start, grow, build, and scale your pop-up shop business, is to combine the launchpads to bring a more unified engagement. Doing so makes an immense difference in the results you will receive while you take your audience on a journey, even as a side hustler before committing to being a startup popupreneur.

Customer expectations are rapidly changing, and businesses need to adapt through physical and digital transformation to understand the customers and their journey. Patron's experience is now becoming the key differentiating factor in their decision-making process and commitment to your business. This can be a positive or negative experience customers receive across the touchpoints. These touchpoints, also referred to as often used launchpads, include e-commerce platforms, startup professionals, physical storefronts, and side hustles (hobbies). Your pop-up shop business will represent any one of these, all, or a combination. How you connect with people at any of these touchpoints is what will eventually define your brand image. The focus of this business literature is how to *"Popup Your E-commerce"*; therefore, for the remainder of this section, the e-commerce touchpoint for tremendous engagement will be the emphasis.

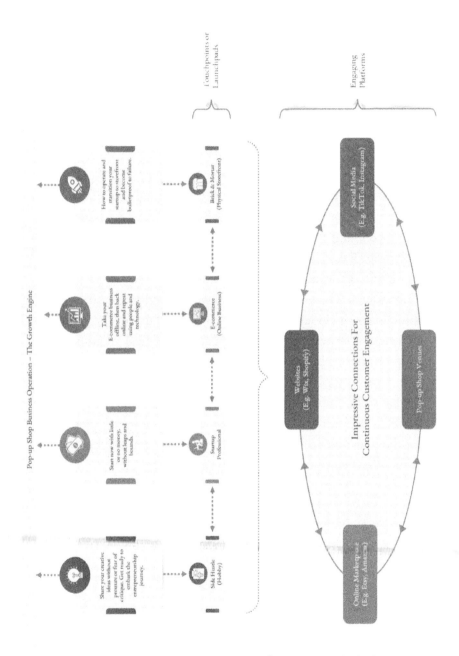

Figure 4. Omnichannel Engagement (The 360° Marketing Life Cycle):
https://www.popupshopbusiness.com/omnichannel-framework-flowchart

At this point, I am sure you are seeing the pattern of how a *Popup Your E-commerce* touchpoint works. As stated before, you will take your online business offline, then back online, and repeat the effort by taking people on a journey using technology as a vehicle or transporter.

Overcoming Fear and Insecurities

The decision to open a pop-up shop was one that I hesitated over for quite some time. Initially, my inclination was to start an online business, as the idea of a physical storefront seemed daunting. Financial limitations aside, my insecurities about interpersonal communication and showcasing my products to potential customers were major roadblocks. I worried that people might question my authenticity, assuming I was not local, or worse, that I didn't belong in the community, given my intention to offer Caribbean-inspired products. These fears were primarily birth from the intimidating thoughts within my own mind rather than reflecting the reality of the situation.

It was my sister Kimoy who encouraged me to venture into the realm of pop-up shops. Without her words of reassurance, this journey might not have existed at all. Her belief in my abilities and the potential of my business idea bolstered my confidence to take that leap of faith.

Next, I shared the idea with my spouse at the time, and to my surprise, she seemed to have been more enthusiastic about it than I was. She was excited to accompany me and share my Caribbean-inspired goods with the local community. However, I still grappled with fear, particularly regarding how I might be perceived during interactions with the locals. My Jamaican accent, which I perceived as awkward, and my tendency to speak rapidly left me concerned that shop guests might not fully understand what I was saying. Additionally, I doubted my skills as a salesperson, questioning whether I could effectively convey the passion I had for my brand and get others excited about it. These doubts led me to consider the outlook of building a successful e-commerce company, where I could avoid direct interactions and simply operate from behind a laptop. As an introvert, I initially thought this option was attractive.

But like many others, I harbored fears of meeting people for the first time, especially at crowded pop-up events. Yet, I realized that taking the first step was necessary. I decided to face my fears and embrace the challenge of the pop-up shop. I pushed myself to do it not just once but multiple times until it became a routine. Through this process, I discovered that as I became more accustomed to the experience, my fears began to gradually dissipate.

Over time, I found my rhythm and confidence in engaging with guests at my pop-up booth. As I repeatedly put myself out there, connecting with customers became more natural and less intimidating. It was a learning curve, but one that proved to be immensely rewarding.

To anyone who may also struggle with fear and insecurity, particularly in the context of selling or engaging with others, I offer this advice: Take that first step, and then take it again. Embrace the challenge, knowing that with each attempt, you will grow more comfortable and proficient. The fears that once held you back will gradually lose their grip, allowing you to find your own way and connect with your audience effortlessly.

My journey from hesitancy to empowerment in running a pop-up shop exemplifies the power of overcoming fear and insecurity. With support from loved ones and the determination to face our anxieties head-on, we can embrace new challenges and ultimately find success. Whether you're an introvert like me or simply someone grappling with self-doubt, remember that growth often lies just beyond the confines of our comfort zones. Embrace the process, and you'll likely find that engaging with others and pursuing your dreams becomes a rewarding and natural part of your business and life.

Engage, Convert, Retain

To attract people to your pop-up events, you need to use a creative online marketing plan that works. It's not just about making announcements; it's a whole process that involves engaging, converting, and retaining your audience. Here are some tools you can use to do it:

Email Marketing – Sending enticing emails to notify your customers about upcoming pop-up events is just the first step. To be successful, you should do more than just announce the events. Start by building and maintaining your list with each pop-up appearance. This email list is of value for connecting with potential attendees and gathering important insights over time.

CRM (Customer Relationship Management) – Having a dedicated CRM system is essential. It helps you not only collect email addresses but also gather information about customer preferences and behaviors. This data enables you to group your audience so you can identify who is interested in your brand.

Tailored Follow-Up – Armed with this knowledge helps with creating highly personalized follow-up campaigns. Your communication should go beyond event reminders. See customer's preferences and purchase history and offer discounts and promotions that match their tastes.

Value-Added Content – In addition to discounts and promotions, share information that educates and entertains. This could include exclusive content related to your products, insights about your industry, or lifestyle tips. Offering such content can turn one-time attendees into faithful followers.

Virtual Engagement – For those who can't physically attend your temporary storefront, use the virtual engagement options. Live streams, virtual tours, or interactive Q&A sessions can help connect a larger group of people.

Building an audience for your venues is not just about sending notifications. It also involves email marketing, using CRM effectively, personalized follow-up, creating valuable content, engaging on social media, and providing virtual accessibility. This attracts crowds and builds a strong community.

PART II

Value Each Person

When running a pop-up stand, it's important to understand how being friendly and using good communication can make your selling more successful. By paying attention to customers who want a positive experience, you can improve your sales efforts. The goal is to make sure every customer feels not just okay but truly valued and respected. You can achieve this by using proper customer service manners, selling with intent, and engaging with people who are just browsing.

Customer Service Etiquette

In the world of sales, good service etiquette helps with a positive and lasting impression with people on the other side of your booth. With that, when running a pop-up shop, here are some things to keep in mind:

Friendly and Appropriate Gestures – Maintain a friendly demeanor and appropriate gestures to ensure customers feel comfortable and respected. Avoid any actions or words that could be misinterpreted.

Valuing Every Client – Treat each person as if they are an esteemed guest. Make them feel extremely satisfied, appreciated, and valued. Remember that they are not just paying customers but individuals seeking a positive experience.

Communication Channels – Once again, encourage customers to reach out via email for any questions or concerns that may arise after their visit. This proactiveness can prevent dissatisfied customers from venting their frustrations in online reviews or social groups.

Training and Mentoring – Invest in training and mentoring for your sales team to instill these customer service behaviors. Your sales-people are the face of your brand, and their interactions significantly impact your business's reputation.

Sell on Purpose

Selling on purpose has become the foundation for building lasting customer relationships. It goes beyond mere transactions; it's about creating meaningfulness. Here, we delve into the art of selling on purpose, where the key focus is satisfying customers' needs.

Overcoming Hesitation – Build trust through transparency. *Imagine this scenario*: a customer shops at your booth but hesitates when asked for their email address. This moment is crucial. It's your chance to showcase your commitment to selling on purpose. Understanding their reservations is the first step. Assure them that their information is an asset, not mere data to be exploited. Transparency is your ally here; emphasize that the information sent to their inbox is meticulously curated, designed to be genuinely helpful, and far from the dreaded spammy clutter.

But it doesn't stop there. Express genuine empathy for their concerns. Understand their perspective and address their fears head-on. Explain, in clear terms, why subscribing to your content will benefit them. Highlight how your emails will provide solutions, offer insights, and enrich their lives. Make them feel valued, not just spenders, but as individuals with unique needs and aspirations.

Engaging Window Shoppers – In the bustling marketplace, not everyone who browses will buy immediately. This is where the true power of selling on purpose shines. Even those who merely window-shop can be converted into long-term advocates. How? By encouraging them to take a simple step: subscribing to your email list.

This seemingly small action has a far-reaching impact. It extends your reach, giving you a direct line of communication with individuals who've expressed an interest in your offerings. These people might not be ready to make a purchase today, but they've shown a curiosity that deserves acknowledgment.

Selling on purpose here means keeping these window shoppers involved. Craft your email content with the intention to inform, inspire, and educate. Share stories, tips, and exclusive insights that relate to their interests. By doing so, you are building a list, as well as nurturing relationships that can bloom into sales when the time is right.

Selling on purpose transcends the traditional sales approach. It's about turning casual observers into loyal customers by providing value and staying connected. When you sell on purpose, you don't just make sales; you create lasting relationships that are the foundation of any business success.

Building a List Matters

Building and maintaining an email list offers several benefits:

Easy Communication – Email lists provide a direct and easy way to reach your customers.

Customer Retention: It helps bring customers back to your temporary shops and online storefront.

Personal Touch: Email marketing allows for a more personalized approach, fostering rapport and trust.

Customer Insights: You can learn about customer behavior and tailor unique advertisements.

Website Traffic Control: Collecting emails helps grow website traffic that you control and retain indefinitely.

Optimizing Email Growth

When your email marketing efforts don't seem to be delivering the results you're hoping for, it's a sign that your current email list might not be predominantly composed of your ideal customers. However, it's important to realize that building your dream audience through email marketing takes time and a well-thought-out planning.

To expand your audience within your email list, the key is to gradually grow the list itself. The idea is simple: as your list grows, so does the potential for your email campaigns to achieve better conversion rates.

There are various things to consider when growing your list of emails. First and foremost, ask all your pop-up guests who are not already on your list to join. Overall, focus on attracting high-quality leads who are more likely to be interested in your offerings. For website visitor appeal, use lead magnets, compelling content, and incentives to encourage potential customers to also subscribe to your list online. Once you've amassed a larger number of email addresses, consider segmenting your list based on factors like demographics, behavior, and preferences. This allows you to send personalized content to specific groups, increasing your chances of conversion.

Remember to keep a consistent communication schedule with your subscribers to keep them interested. Regularly analyze the performance of your email campaigns and adjust your approach based on what resonates best with your audience. Encourage your existing subscribers to refer others who may also be interested; word-of-mouth referrals can be quite powerful. Utilize your social media to promote your email sign-up and invite your followers to join your list, as cross-promotion can help you attract new subscribers.

Lastly, don't hesitate to experiment with different aspects of your emails, such as subject lines, content formats, and calls-to-action. This experimentation can help you fine-tune your emails for maximum engagement and conversions.

Growing your list and expanding your dream audience is an ongoing process. While it may take time, with a strategic and persistent effort, you can gradually increase the number of ideal customers on your list, leading to improved email marketing performance.

Running a successful pop-up shop involves more than just setting up a temporary retail space and displaying your products. To maximize your sales and create a memorable shopping experience, understand the different types of people who are likely to buy from your shop. By identifying your dream customers, local shoppers, and curious buyers, you can tailor your marketing plans and product offerings to cater to their specific needs.

Committed Engagers

Committed engagers are typical characteristics of dream customers. They are the backbone of any successful pop-up shop. These individuals are passionate about your brand and, in most cases, also a part of your target audience. They are the ones who eagerly anticipate your pop-up events and are more likely to make significant purchases. Here are some of their characteristics:

Dream Diehard Fans

Brand Loyalty – Dream diehard fans exhibit firm loyalty. They may follow you on social media, sign up for newsletters, and attend your pop-up shops whenever possible.

Example Scenario: A clothing brand's diehard fans eagerly await its seasonal pop-up shop to get the latest designs and limited-edition items.

Repeat Purchases – Your dream fans are likely to make repeat purchases, become advocates, and spread the word to friends and family.

Example Scenario: A gourmet chocolate brand's loyal customers attend every pop-up shop to stock up on their favorite chocolates and advocate new flavors to friends.

Super Engagers – They engage with your brand beyond just buying products, participating in contests, sharing user-generated content, and providing feedback.

Example Scenario: A local artisan jewelry brand's dream fan actively participates in Instagram photo contests featuring their products.

Local Supporters

Local shoppers are a significant segment of your pop-up shop's potential super-engagers. They prioritize supporting local businesses and are more inclined to explore new products and brands in their community. Key characteristics of local shoppers include:

Community-Centric – Local shoppers are deeply rooted in their community and are committed to helping local startups thrive.

Example Scenario: A pop-up shop showcasing handmade pottery receives a steady stream of local customers eager to promote local craftsmanship.

Product Discovery: They are open to discovering new and unique products, especially those created by local artisans and entrepreneurs.

Example Scenario: A local artisanal pop-up food truck attracts customers interested in trying unique and locally sourced culinary delights.

Building Relationships: Local shoppers value building relationships with local business owners and appreciate the personal touch of a pop-up shop experience.

Example Scenario: A pop-up bookstore offers book signings and author meet-and-greets, drawing in local book enthusiasts.

Curious Eager Buyers

Curious buyers represent a versatile group of potential customers for your temporary shop. They may not be familiar with your brand or products but are excited to explore. Here are some characteristics of curious buyers:

Open-Minded: Curious buyers have an open-minded approach to shopping and are willing to try products or brands they haven't encountered before.

Example Scenario: A pop-up shop featuring innovative tech gadgets attracts customers interested in exploring the latest technology.

Product Sampling: They are receptive to product samples, demos, and interactive experiences that allow them to test and understand your products better.

Example Scenario: A skincare brand offers free skincare consultations and samples at their pop-up, attracting customers curious about skincare solutions.

Potential Dream Customers: Over time, curious buyers can transform into dream diehard fans if they have a positive first experience with your company.

Example Scenario: A pop-up shop offering unique handcrafted candles piques the interest of curious buyers, some of whom become loyal customers after trying the products.

Before you begin reading the next guide on how to attract more people online, let's talk about something important: making sure those who've attended your events don't forget about your brand. It's all about staying connected with them. Keeping in touch and building rapport can turn those who bought from you once into loyal, long-term customers.

Understanding the different kinds of people who support your pop-up business is key. Whether you're catering to your dream diehard fans, folks from your local area, or just people who are curious, each group has its own unique preferences and expectations. By recognizing and engaging with these different customer groups, you can boost sales, build strong customer loyalty, and create a shopping experience they won't forget—one that keeps them coming back for more.

So, with this in mind, let's move on to the next secret for more ways to bring traffic to your online business and seal your digital authority.

CUSTOMER ENGAGMEMENT WORKSHEET
– Deliver the Full Experience.

1. What does omnichannel engagement mean, and why is it essential for a pop-up shop business?

_____

_____

_____

_____

_____

2. How does the 360-degree marketing strategy contribute to the omnichannel approach?

_____

_____

_____

_____

_____

3. In the context of engaging with customers, what are your fears or reservations, if any?

_____

_____

_____

_____

_____

4. Define the concept of selling on purpose based on the information provided.

_____

_____

_____

_____

_____

SECRET GUIDE #5

Direct Traffic to your Online Brand

Flood your Online Places with People and Garner Credibility.

Bridging the Gap

Once you've put in the time and effort to create and improve your online store, the next step is to get people to visit it in abundance. While digital marketing is essential for driving online traffic, offline pop-up events build meaningful customer relationships. In this guide, I'll show you how e-commerce and online business owners can make the most of pop-up shops by directing customers to their online storefronts. I'll reveal how to get lots of visitors to your website and enhance your credibility by bridging the gap.

Engaging with customers isn't just about talking to them in person at your pop-up storefront. These encounters are also used to direct shop guests to your website. One effective way to do this is to create a bridge between your website and online marketplaces with your temporary shops. You do this by prominently displaying your web address, social media profiles, and QR codes that lead visitors directly to where you want them to go over the internet. Now, if you're an experienced vendor or have been following my earlier advice, you might already have these fundamentals in place to some extent. Because what I've noticed is that merely having these scannable QR codes and website links on display at your table or booth isn't enough. You need to actively encourage shop visitors to use them. Just having them there won't cut it. You must guide people who stop at your booth to scan, click, and share these links. Without this active approach, the connection between your physical pop-up and virtual storefronts won't work as it should. Here, next, I will explain:

Sales Process Guide

Guiding your pop-up shop visitors through a sales process is what you should use for everyone who visits, whether they're thinking of buying something or not. This is important for directing people online and building virtual relationships. Here's the step-by-step guide to this process:

Step 1: Welcoming Interaction – When people come to your temporary shop, it all begins here. Regardless of whether they're regular customers or new to your shop, follow this sequence, especially for newcomers.

Step 2: Starting a Conversation – When someone comes to your booth and doesn't know much about your company, they may ask questions about what you offer. Your sales team should respond with a clear and enticing value statement about your products, like "We have natural healing organic skincare products!" This brief statement must describe how your products can make their lives better and address their specific needs. It must also show how your products fulfill one of the core desires of your target audience: health, wealth, or better relationships.

Step 3: Assessing the Value Proposition – After sharing your value statement, potential buyers will consider whether your product can meet their needs or benefit someone they know. Some people may become advocates for your brand even if they don't find a direct solution for themselves.

Step 4: Imagining Use or Enjoyment – Following your explained value, prospects might start imagining how they could use or enjoy your product(s) or service(s). If it fits their needs or desires, they're more likely to make a purchase.

Step 5: Features, Benefits, Attributes (FAB) – Before making a purchase, prospects may also want to know more about the product, like its ingredients, how to use it, and how it aligns with the value statement you provided earlier.

Step 6: Closing the Sale – After these conversations, many pop-up guests are likely to make a purchase. During the transaction, you can suggest additional items or deals to help them save money, like bundle kits or special discounts.

Step 7: Scan and Share – After a purchase or not, make sure to ask customers to scan QR codes and share your brand information with others. Some may decline, so be persuasive but not pushy.

Step 8: Email List Signup – Encourage them to join your email list after scanning and sharing. If they're hesitant to share their contact info, that's okay; the goal is to confidently ask for these actions to keep them connected and provide updates about your products and services.

In short, this eight-step process involves welcoming visitors with your value proposal, encouraging purchases, requesting scans and shares, and finally, urging them to sign up for your email list. This ensures you can continue helping them while keeping them engaged and informed.

When you're talking to customers at an event that has supported your business, it's important to give them full access to your company online. Share your brand message, provide links to customer reviews, and make valuable content on your website easily accessible. My experience has shown that most people will happily follow your guide, so these are not outrageous requests. By showcasing the reliability and value of your online brand during face-to-face conversation, you reassure and encourage pop-up guests to go further and make future purchases online.

It has become almost instinctive for customers to verify a business's credibility on the internet before proceeding with additional purchases or an initial commitment. In recognizing this, guide them online while they're enjoying their pop-up shopping experience. Being proactive increases traffic to your website and social media, enhancing greater familiarity with your business.

Consistently guiding people at your booth in this way will naturally move your grassroots efforts into virtual fireworks. When you significantly bridge the gap between your offline and online, you create a digital harmony that ensures a successful and lasting connection beyond the confines of your pop-up shop operations.

A Symphony of Digital Harmonies

In this part, I've simplified the "*Popup Your E-commerce*" framework to cater to those who might feel overwhelmed by online business operations. Here I am highlighting how these elements tie together to enhance your pop-up shop's online presence. Basically, the material shared in this part summarizes this book. However, this section will not be enough for you to master such a framework. So please read on and enhance your knowledge with a few more vital pieces of information.

As explained previously, extending your pop-up shop's reach, generally guides your in-person visitors toward ensuing online interactions. Let's look at a few user-friendly online avenues that can help you achieve just that:

Website (E-commerce or Online Business) – A website, the cornerstone of your online authority, houses an array of web pages, images, and digital assets. This virtual storefront beckons customers with information, products, or services. Embrace the power of an e-commerce site or an online business to showcase your offerings, ensuring a lasting digital impression.

Amplify Your Popularity with Social Media: Use your social media as your megaphone in the virtual realm. Social places like Facebook, Twitter, Instagram, TikTok, LinkedIn, and YouTube amplify the exchange of ideas, information, and content. These digital hangouts allow you to engage with a broader audience, cultivating relationships and visibility.

Expand Your Digital Market Reach Online Marketplace: Think of an online marketplace as a bustling web bazaar where commerce thrives. Amazon, eBay, and Etsy exemplify this concept, enabling the buying and selling of products and services with ease. Mirror the real-world marketplace experience, harnessing the internet to connect with a vast array of customers.

Crafting Customer Journeys with Click-Funnels: Click-Funnels emerges as a game-changer. Think of it as your digital toolkit for creating visually appealing landing pages, sales pages, and comprehensive marketing funnels. This platform simplifies the process, allowing you to engage potential customers effortlessly. With templates and drag-and-drop tools at your disposal, you can effortlessly sculpt high-conversion pathways. Click-Funnels integrates with email marketing and payment systems, streamlining your sales strategy. The ultimate objective? Empowering businesses to captivate, convert, and close deals with finesse.

Storytelling Engages and Elevates with Vlogs and Blogs: Become the go-to expert by embracing the world of vlogs and blogs. A blog, akin to an online journal, offers insights, opinions, and personal experiences. It's where you can establish credibility and engage in conversations with your audience. On the other hand, a vlog (video blog) takes you a step further, using dynamic videos to share knowledge, tutorials, reviews, and more. This medium brings your expertise to life, offering a more interactive and worthwhile journey.

By intertwining these online pathways, you empower your pop-up shop customers to transition over the internet. Whether through funnels, an engaging website, vibrant social media interactions, virtual marketplace ventures, or compelling vlogs and blogs, you're orchestrating a symphony of online engagement with modern consumers. Your pop-up shop doesn't just stop at the physical; it extends into the digital web.

Extending the Pop-Up Magic Online

Amid the bustling interactions and vibrant transactions of your pop-up shop, some patrons may find themselves yearning for more. This transition from physical dealings to virtual forms the crux of post-pop-up rendezvous. If needed, review the prior secret and continue to navigate the art of guiding your pop-up visitors toward your e-commerce stores, where inquiries, feedback, and purchases flourish, creating new waves of interest that rejuvenate your brand.

Traffic Strategies

So far, some of my previous discussions have gone deeply into site traffic, examining both its offline and online manifestations. We've explored various categories of traffic, ranging from SEO and digital contexts to the engagement generated by interactions in physical pop-up shops. Now, let's consolidate and elucidate some diverse traffic types, encompassing both online avenues and offline venue operations. This overview aims to enhance your comprehension of when and how these traffic strategies come into play as you elevate your E-commerce endeavors through pop-up shops.

Organic Traffic – Aim to attain and maintain this type of traffic. The heart of website visits is organic traffic—the visitors who land on your site through unpaid search engine results. These individuals, driven by their search for keywords related to your content or services, symbolize a high-quality audience with genuine interest and a strong intent to engage and convert.

Direct Traffic – Direct traffic emerges from users directly inputting your website URL or clicking a bookmark. This signifies a personal connection or prior engagement with your business online. As your pop-up shop entices visitors, it prominently displays printed signs, website URLs, and QR codes. These QR codes, when scanned, guide visitors to valuable web content, enhancing engagement and facilitating activities like coupon redemption and amplified social media reach. If you follow the advice in this secret guide, you should be able to direct traffic to your website without any trouble.

Paid Traffic – Paid traffic involves advertising efforts to propel your visitors online. Through channels like search engines, social media, or display networks, advertisers pay to target specific demographics, locations, or interests. The objective here is to achieve heightened conversions, leads, and ROI (Return on Investment) compared to other digital marketing strategies.

Social Media Engagement – Leverage social media for engagement and interaction with your patrons, as discussed in Secret Guide #4. Encourage them to take photos of your pop-up booth, products, and website URL, as I have explained in the previous guide. Promptly respond to their reviews, likes, and shares, urging them to follow your business pages and online communities. This social rapport ensures continued connection beyond the pop-up event's conclusion.

Building an Email List for Owned Traffic – Recognize the importance of an email list as a conduit for owned traffic. Your list empowers you to channel substantial traffic to your E-commerce storefront, a traffic stream under your control. Unlike other sources like organic, direct, paid, or social media, this traffic comes from the emails you send directly to people's inboxes. With a well-executed pop-up shop engagement, you can accumulate thousands of emails through events, granting you a formidable arsenal for future online promotions and sales.

Imagine the potency of harnessing your list of 52,000 contacts in a couple of years. A single email campaign featuring a $50 product could yield staggering returns. Even a conservative 1% conversion rate translates to an instant $26,000. By nurturing and expanding your list over time, your revenue potential skyrockets, making the initial effort incredibly worthwhile.

The synergy of these traffic generation techniques emerges at your pop-up booth, where you gather email addresses for marketing, optimize organic SEO efforts, employ direct traffic through QR codes and URLs, and occasionally deploy paid ads on platforms like Microsoft Bing, Facebook, and Google.

In essence, your mastery of these traffic avenues—organic, direct, paid, and owned—positions you to navigate E-commerce flawlessly. Balancing your web-based optimization endeavors with the tangible engagement of offline pop-up shops, you orchestrate a symphony of traffic, propelling your business toward remarkable success.

E-Commerce Orchestration

In "*Popup Your E-commerce*," every note that plays vibrates with a harmonious blend of strategies, much like the symphonies of Beethoven and the enchanting melodies of Paganini. While my personal talents may not lie in classical musical instruments, I find a kinship in the art of orchestrating the digital realm, inspired by the likes of a Newport News mid-week farmers market pop-up shop merchant.

Just as a fellow popupreneur's melodies stirred a resonance within me, so too does the notion of an orchestrated symphony in the land of pop-up shops. Imagine the calm, confident, and patient guidance that unfolds as you guide visitors through the ebbs and flows of your pop-up shop. With the same artistry as the greats, you direct the rhythm, connecting with individuals and sending them on an omnichannel journey that transcends the physical confines of your storefront.

From the resonant chords of engagement at your temporary venue to the crescendo of online meetings, as visitors explore your website, each step is a carefully composed movement. The QR code and social shares become a bridge, transporting them from the tangible to the digital, and as they reach the crescendo of the checkout stage, transactions become the grand finale of this symphonic narrative.

But this journey doesn't end with the closing notes of a sale. Like a lingering melody, the connection endures. The online avenues you've deftly introduced serve as the refrain, inviting guests to continue their exploration. It's a melody that echoes beyond the pop-up, evolving into future online purchases.

As the secret of directing traffic to your online brand draws to a close, remember the lessons of the masters—Beethoven's patience, da Vinci's innovation, and Paganini's virtuosity. Your approach is no different—a harmonious blend of confidence, patience, and a meticulous orchestration of the omni-channel experience. With each calculated note, you shape the e-commerce journey, which stays in the minds of your audience and harmonizes with the information age.

And now, as the final chords of this secret guide fade, we turn our attention to the next stage of your symphony: "Follow-up and Build Rapport." Just as a maestro skillfully maintains the momentum and intrigue between movements, you'll discover how to cultivate lasting impact, nurture relationships, and create an ongoing dialogue that echoes through time. Let the journey continue as you learn the art of building rapport and establishing a harmonious bond with your audience.

DIRECT TRAFFIC ONLINE WORKSEET –
Lead People Where You Want Them to Go.

1. Why is it emphasized in the guide that merely having QR codes and website links on display isn't enough? What is the additional step recommended?

_____

_____

_____

_____

_____

2. Explain the eight-step sales process guide outlined in the text. How does it contribute to bridging the gap between offline and online interactions?

_____

_____

_____

_____

_____

SECRET GUIDE #6
Follow-Up and Build Rapport

Nurture Relationships Online Following Your Pop-up Shop Efforts.

PART I

In modern commerce, establishing genuine connections with customers is supreme. As you churn into the pages of this secret guide, titled "Follow-Up and Build Rapport, Nurture Relationships Online Following Your Pop-up Shop Efforts," you will go further on a journey that extends beyond the confines of a physical shop.

In a world where online exchanges and virtual experiences hold considerable sway, the art of nurturing relationships takes on new dimensions. Here, unraveled are the intricacies of post-pop-up shops, learning ways to foster lasting rapport with your audience, from personalized follow-ups to cultivating a dynamic online existence. This secret will be your guidepost for making a lasting impact long after your pop-up shop has ended.

Pop-Up to Digital

In this age of interconnectedness, just assuming an online presence is no longer satisfactory. It is now mandatory to blend your pop-up encounters with your digital imprint. The key to untying much of this mystery lies in devising strategies that guarantee each visitor departing from your booth remains keenly conscious of your online channels, solidifying a cohesive identity that bridges the gap between the tangible and virtual persistently.

Popup Your E-commerce Symphony

Envision your pop-ups as the gateway to a journey, a carefully crafted funnel designed to guide customers toward conversion, whether it's a sale, signup, or any desired action. As you and your skilled sales managers engage visitors at your booths, you orchestrate an experience that transitions them through each step of the funnel. Below are the stages of this funnel, which will also be depicted in the accompanying diagram.

Step 1: Pop-up shop Venue – Igniting the Journey: At the heart of it all is your pop-up shop venue, *The Business Growth Engine*," a space where your team engages with customers in person. This physical interaction sparks the journey, drawing visitors into your world of offerings and possibilities.

Step 2: Website Homepage or Landing Pages – Unveiling Your Brand: The first digital note in the symphony is struck as customers are directed to your website's homepage or specific landing pages. Here, they delve deeper into your brand's story, essence, and ethos. Attractive visuals and compelling narratives unfold, enticing them to explore further.

Step 3: Product Page – The Heart of Offerings: With curiosity piqued, customers navigate to the product page. This step is triggered by scanning a QR code, granting them access to comprehensive information about a specific merchandise or a service. They can make informed decisions whether to purchase online or carry the enthusiasm to an offline experience.

Step 4: Checkout – Sealing the Deal: For those ready to make an immediate purchase, the checkout stage awaits. It's the crescendo of the funnel, where customers seal the deal and take the desired action. Whether it's a product, service, or subscription, this is where transactions come to life.

Step 5: Future Online Purchases – Sustaining the Connection: But the symphony doesn't end here. The experience you've orchestrated leaves an indelible mark. Customers, armed with newfound knowledge and a connection to your brand, continue to make future purchases online. Whether it's a repeat visit to the website, exploring more products, or engaging with your offerings via other online avenues, the momentum continues.

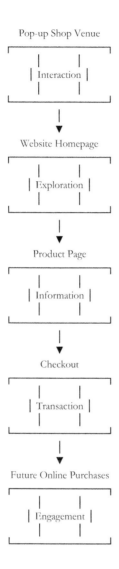

Figure 5. Popup Your E-commerce Symphony.

In this orchestrated symphony, you guide your pop-up shop customers from in-person interactions to a harmonious blend of digital engagement and conversions. The funnel's stages flow, ensuring that every interaction enhances their connection with your company, leading to nonstop online visits and future purchases.

Dynamic Social Media

Social media serves as digital amphitheaters, offering a dynamic space where your audience not only participates but also extends warm invitations to their friends. This allows them to fully enjoy the excitement of your pop-up events and real-time posts. Within this lively online realm, you have the chance to harness the complete potential of these platforms, transforming them into thriving hubs.

From captivating interactive pop-up experiences that immerse participants in unforgettable moments to crafting a virtual domain that shifts into vibrant social arenas of engagement, the opportunities are limitless. Your skilled sales force serves as the driving engine behind these efforts, which in turn elevates your company's status. This guarantees that your business becomes a central point of discussions characterized by a flurry of shares, likes, and follows—interactions that continue long after the final curtain falls on your events.

Timeless Blog Narratives

As you navigate the digital interface, the powerful avenue of blogging resurfaces as an online marketing tool. "Blogging Your Brand: Crafting Informative Narratives for Online Audiences" reveals the art of creating compelling narratives that appeal to readers and establish your brand as a credible voice in your industry over the long term.

In blogging, telling a great story is incredibly important. Think of your brand like an unknown novel, and your well-crafted blog posts act as guiding lights for people who are curious. These posts offer deep insights into your business.

If you've tried out my techniques for creating effective and well-written blogs, you've probably started to see more people visiting your blog naturally. These stories aren't just ordinary words—they're a part of the strategies that help your content show up on search engines organically, promote your brand, and reach people through email campaigns. They work like a roadmap, leading people from their emails, QR code scans, social media, or search engine results to the amazing solutions you provide with written content.

Ultimately, the aim is to become skilled at creating engaging articles and newsletters. These shouldn't just give information; they should also grab people's attention and make them feel a sense of fulfilment. These actions, built over time, create a trust that goes beyond the current moment and keeps resonating as you keep sharing new blog posts.

A classic blog that remains relevant throughout time is like a treasure trove of information that builds rapport. To achieve this, here are a list of important things to consider:

Timeless Topics – Instead of focusing on short-lived trends, these blogs talk about subjects that are always important. These topics stay helpful no matter when your visitors read them.

Good Writing – Well-written content with clear language and interesting stories is powerful. It makes the blog trustworthy and easy to read. If you happen to be a subpar writer, there are plenty of writing tools, like Grammarly, that can assist.

Storytelling – Stories connect with people emotionally. Adding personal stories and examples to the content makes it relatable and memorable.

Useful Information – These blogs offer practical advice or solutions that your audience can potentially use. They help with common problems and answer questions so readers trust them.

Pictures and Videos – Adding images, charts, or videos that make sense improves the blog's looks and helps explain things better. It also gives readers a chance to pause and relax so the reading material is not so daunting to read. Lengthier blogs must have photos and videos.

Relevant Keywords – Including important words that stay relevant over time, i.e., keywords or keyword phrases, helps the blog show up in search engines. This way, people can find it whenever they need to on SERP.

Keep It Up – Publishing good content regularly builds trust and shows that the blog is a reliable source.

Think About the Readers – Writing about things that matter to the people reading the blog, especially the target audience you serve, keeps it interesting and helpful.

Stay Away From Trends – Avoid using words or references that might not make sense in the future. This keeps the blog from getting old quickly.

Keep It Fresh – Reviewing and updating the content ensures that it's accurate and still useful, even after a long time.

By following the above-listed advice, blogs become a source of information that lasts. They continue to be useful and wise for a long time, even after they were first written.

Furthermore, blogs must deliver value to readers. They are like digital journals where businesses address common challenges, give solutions, offer guidance, and share industry insights. By regularly creating useful and informative content, you quench your customers' thirst for knowledge and establish yourself as a reliable source of advice. This positive cycle builds strong loyalty and rapport and ensures readers are happy.

Power of Blogging

Do you want to strengthen how you connect with your customers? Blogging might be the solution. By now, you've probably been updating your previous blogs or creating new ones. I've talked a lot about blogging in general, and I hope you're starting to see its value like I do.

Many entrepreneurs underestimated the potential of this digital marketing tool when social media gained popularity. They believed that people wouldn't enjoy reading or engaging with blog content. However, as I've previously explained, if you approach it correctly, you can effectively engage readers through well-organized written content, as shown in Secret Guide #2. If you're still uncertain, allow me to elaborate on how blogging can truly benefit your business.

Improving Your Search Engine Rankings – It's no secret that SEO is important online, and blogs play a big role in it. When you provide fresh and relevant content, of course your search engine rankings get better. By using the right keywords, correct meta tags, and smart linking, your blogs will show up higher in search results. This means more people will find your content and visit your site.

Getting More People to Visit Your Website – Blogging obviously brings more visitors to your website. When you regularly publish high-quality content that search engines like, your website becomes more visible and ranks higher in search results. As more people discover your brand through your blogs, you increase the chances to build rapport and eventually turn them into loyal customers.

Getting Leads and Turning Them into Customers – Blogs are means for getting leads and convincing them to become customers. Offer content that encourages readers to share their information, often in exchange for exclusive resources. After that, you can guide these leads through the sales process, which helps with revenue growth.

Becoming an Expert in Your Industry – Begin your blogging journey to become a respected leader in your field. By sharing useful and informative content, you're not only showing your expertise but also establishing yourself as someone people can bond with. This helps build trust and respect from your customers and competitors, making your reputation stronger.

Adding blogging to your business plan can really boost how you connect with customers, establish your expertise, and contribute to the growth of your business. I've talked about this in more detail in previous sections, so feel free to revisit them if you need a reminder about some points.

As you've gained much understanding of blogging's transformative potential, let's pivot to another powerful strategy that complements the timeless and powerful narratives we've explored so far. Just as blogs serve as the source of customer communication, they also align with grassroots marketing—a strategy that nurtures authentic connections through organic means. By mixing the art of storytelling with accepting feedback, your business will not only establish itself as a trusted advisor but also promote genuine relationships. So, let's uncover the workings of the balancing act in customer feedback.

Customer Reviews

Creating an environment where customers feel comfortable sharing their experiences, whether on your website or in a review on Google or Trustpilot, is key. By understanding how these reviews impact online interactions and guiding customers to give feedback, you show how these opinions can attract new customers and build a fan base.

Balancing Act in Customer Feedback

Even though the internet is powerful, we shouldn't forget how effective grassroots marketing can be. If you have an online business with pop-up shops or plan to start one, it's important to learn how to naturally attract customers. Do this by making professional friends with people you meet at events and using these networks to build a strong foundation for your business to succeed.

When you combine meeting people in person with your online efforts, it helps your business grow progressively. It also shows how valuable it is to get different opinions that can guide your pop-up shop to success. So, stay in touch with customers and form good relationships with them. Doing this is the first step to getting continuing favorable ratings.

Diversified Feedback

In your pop-up shop's interactions with customers, how they engage with your business takes an interesting turn when it comes to their feedback ratings. These opinions from shoppers can propel your business forward and help potential customers decide whether to do business with you. Your goal is to build a great reputation, but aiming for only perfect five-star ratings might not always be the best approach. It's sometimes ok to accept a range of feedback, from three to five stars, on different platforms.

It's tempting to imagine a scenario where every review you get is glowing with five stars. But it's important to realize that from a potential customer's perspective, this doesn't necessarily mean your business is perfect. Here's why my viewpoint on this matters:

Lack of Authenticity – If your business only has perfect five-star ratings, it might make customers skeptical. In a world where people expect a variety of opinions and experiences, not having any negative feedback might make people doubt if those reviews are genuine.

Unrealistic Expectations – Relying only on five star reviews might set unrealistic standards for potential customers. When everything seems perfect, customers might expect every aspect of their experience to be flawless. If their actual experience falls short, they might end up disappointed.

Limited Insights – Negative reviews and constructive criticism can be helpful for improving your products and services. If you only get positive feedback, you might miss out on chances to identify and fix areas that need improvement.

Diverse Preferences – Customers have a wide range of preferences. A five-star review might represent an amazing experience for one customer, but it might not align with another customer's unique expectations. Different reviews help potential customers decide if your business suits their personal preferences.

Suspicion of Manipulation – In a world where fake reviews are a concern, having only perfect five-star ratings could make people skeptical. They might wonder if the reviews are manipulated or fake, which could undermine their trust in your business.

Tailored Experiences – Customers judge products and services based on various criteria. A five-star review might highlight things that matter a lot to one person, but those might not be as important to someone else. Having a mix of reviews gives a more complete picture of what your business offers.

Honesty and Trust – Building trust between your business and customers is important. Having a mix of reviews, both positive and constructive, shows that you're open to feedback and committed to improving.

While five-star reviews are nice, having diverse feedback that includes both praise and criticism gives a more balanced and detailed view of your business's strengths and areas for improvement. This broader perspective helps customers make informed choices.

Building Reviews

If you're looking to connect with consumers and gather their opinions, you've probably been using various methods like blogs, social media, and newsletters. Here, I'll introduce a simple way to get more customer feedback and reviews in a place of your choice. This method is particularly useful if you're aiming to increase reviews.

Step 1: Choosing Your Review Growth Location – You might wonder where to start growing your reviews. The good news is it's up to your business strategy. Whether it's through search engines or elsewhere, the choice is yours. But if you're aiming for more reviews, I suggest starting with search engines, especially Google.

Step 2: Simple Review Collection – Imagine you're at your pop-up booth, and you want to gather reviews intentionally. It's straightforward. Here's how:

> ➤ Every member of your sales team should ask customers to scan a QR code.

> ➤ This code takes them directly to where they can leave a review.

It's that simple!

Step 3: Encouraging Honest Feedback – Not everyone might say yes to leaving a review, and that's perfectly fine. If your product and customer service are great, some people will happily agree. The key is to politely ask your pop-up shop guests to share their honest thoughts about their experience with you.

Something interesting happens when a customer helps your business once—they're more likely to do it again. This includes things like inviting them to read your newsletter about the latest and greatest going on in your company. So, remember that each small interaction can lead to more engagement.

If you're seeking more customer feedback and reviews, remember these easy steps: choose where you want reviews to grow, make use of QR codes, and ask for honest feedback. Plus, keep in mind that engaging with customers in small ways can lead to even greater connections, like inviting them to stay updated with your newsletter.

Newsletters

Let's look at another resource that is impactful online: Newsletters have evolved into a means of establishing a deep connection. Through email marketing, you engage your subscriber base and deliver content. In this part, you will begin to understand the role that newsletters play in enhancing customer communication. Here I have given you six things that can transform these digital messages into powerful relationship-building tools.

Exclusivity and Relevance – Newsletters serve as a channel to provide your subscribers with exclusive, tailored content that peeks at their interests. By carefully curating articles, insights, and resources that appeal to individual preferences, showcase your expertise, and offer genuine value to your readers. This personalization cultivates appreciation and encourages a stronger connection between your brand and subscribers.

Personalization – The art of personalization is a cornerstone in nurturing bonding. Utilizing advanced email marketing tools, can segment your subscriber lists and send customized newsletters that reflect each recipient's preferences, behaviors, and demographics. Personal touches, such as addressing subscribers by name and providing tailored recommendations, elevate the customer experience and further authenticate rapport.

Promotions and Discounts – Newsletters are a potent avenue for unveiling exclusive promotions, discounts, and early access to new rollouts. By extending these special offers to your subscribers, you show acknowledgment of their loyalty and incentivize purchases. This dual effect can drive sales and create a sense of privilege, positioning your subscribers as valued members of an exclusive community.

Company News and Events – Effectively utilizing newsletters involves more than just sharing content – they also serve as a stage for sharing company updates, news, and upcoming events. Whether you're announcing product launches, commemorating milestones, or spotlighting industry developments, newsletters serve as a tether that keeps your email subscribers informed and closely connected to your organization's journey.

Consistency and Timeliness – The foundation of a successful newsletter lies in maintaining consistency and timeliness. By adhering to a regular publication schedule, you underscore your commitment to keeping your readers informed. Strategically timing your newsletter deliveries to consider factors like time zones and subscriber likings ensures optimal engagement. This dedication to punctuality enhances credibility.

Encouraging Action – Newsletters are more than just a means of sharing information—they are a promoter for active engagement. By including compelling calls to action and inviting feedback, you create an open invitation for subscribers to voice their thoughts, opinions, and experiences. This feedback is helpful for refining your offerings and services while building an involved community of people. Additionally, encouraging subscribers to share your newsletters can expand your reach, potentially attracting more site visitors.

Newsletters emerge as steadfast for businesses to connect with their customer base. By delivering exclusive content, infusing personalization, offering special promotions, and keeping subscribers informed, you strengthen customer relationships and boost business objectives. As you realize the full potential of newsletters, you'll witness the formation of a dedicated and engaged subscriber community, eventually driving long-term prosperity.

Your website is now experiencing a sudden influx of traffic due to your dedicated efforts in both operating your pop-up shop and effectively managing online marketing strategies such as newsletters and blogs. This increased activity has led to a boost in your Domain Authority, attracting more attention from individuals interested in your company. This growth has been substantial, prompting a desire to impart your knowledge and experience to others, much like how I am assisting you with my book series, business development services, and training courses.

As a result of your hard work, you have become a recognized leader in your specific niche. Now, you're looking to share your expertise with others. To accomplish this, I recommend that you launch a comprehensive training program or course centered around your area of proficiency. This will allow you to provide guidance to aspiring individuals who are eager to follow a similar path. By sharing your knowledge through a structured training

curriculum, you create a profound impact and contribute posi-
tively to your industry.

PART II

Online Training and Coaching

The digital age has revolutionized how we access knowledge and embrace growth. Online training courses and coaching have emerged as dynamic contributions to a diverse range of educational opportunities and services through the internet. These cater perfectly to both individuals and companies seeking accessible and impactful methods to enhance skills and expertise. In the following sections, I will discuss online training and coaching, exploring their advantages and how they facilitate connections between businesses and clientele.

A Multitude of Learning Pathways – Online training courses and coaching programs span an extensive array of subjects and proficiencies, ensuring learners find content that meets their objectives. Whether it's acquiring technical mastery, refining soft skills, or broadening industry insights, the online is a treasure trove of educational resources. Through platforms like websites, mobile apps, and learning management systems (LMS), participants can dive into these courses at their own pace, anytime and anywhere, making it an ideal fit for busy professionals aiming to advance their careers or basic self-help tips.

Knowledge Sharing – A benefit of online training lies in their ability to provide education and skill enhancement. In delivering well-structured, comprehensive courses, businesses showcase their know-how and dedication to assisting customers in achieving success. This creates a bedrock of trust and reliability, positioning the business as a dependable authority in its specific area.

Sense of Belonging – Online education initiatives possess a unique capacity to build a community among participants. Through interactive forums, collaborative projects, and joint learning activities, learners can interact and exchange insights. This nurtures a supportive milieu where individuals can learn from peers, exchange experiences, and gain diverse perspectives. The sense of camaraderie nurtured within these programs motivates participants to engage actively, enhancing the overall learning journey.

Tailored Guidance and Support – In contrast to conventional classroom settings, online training offers individualized attention and support to learners. Via methods such as personalized coaching sessions, mentorship initiatives, and customized feedback, participants benefit from personalized guidance that addresses their specific requirements. This tailored approach ensures participants feel valued and supported throughout their learning venture. By catering to the unique needs of each learner, your business can provide an enriched learning experience, allowing individuals to unlock their full potential.

Bidirectional Communication – Here you will begin to emphasize interactive communication, empowering learners to engage with you as instructor and fellow participants. This open avenue of communication encourages the exchange of ideas, clarification of concepts, and collaborative problem-solving. Learners can seek guidance from instructors and receive timely responses to queries, resulting in a deeper comprehension of the subject matter. By creating an environment of dialogue, these initiatives facilitate a vibrant learning experience that promotes active involvement and knowledge exchange.

Erecting Trust and Authority – The provision of top-tier content and guidance is paramount in online training and coaching. By offering well-crafted courses, businesses establish trust and authority. Learners acknowledge the value of the knowledge imparted and the prowess of the instructors, reinforcing their confidence in the business's offerings. Furthermore, positive word-of-mouth endorsements from satisfied learners bolster the business's reputation, drawing in more customers and expanding its influence.

Online training has metamorphosed the educational panorama, delivering accessible and effective avenues for individual and company growth and development. Through valuable education, community building, personalized guidance, interactive communication, and trust-building, your business can establish connections with clientele while offering impactful learning. This transformative method of education is a substance for progress and success in modern entrepreneurship.

Share your Expertise

If you are one of the few who have garnered significant skills in your field, you can create educational programs for individuals seeking to learn from you. Here's a guide on how to do so:

Identify Your Niche – Begin by identifying the specific niche or area within your industry where you have excelled. Pinpoint the unique skills, insights, or strategies that set you apart. This specialization will form the core of your training content.

Define Learning Objectives – Outline clear learning objectives for your courses. What do you want participants to achieve by the end of the program? Defining specific goals will help you structure your content effectively.

Structure Course Content – Break down your expertise into manageable modules or lessons. Create a logical flow that gradually builds participants' knowledge and skills. Use real-world examples and case studies to illustrate concepts.

Engage Through Interactive Content – Incorporate diverse content formats, such as video lectures, quizzes, assignments, and interactive discussions. Engaging content keeps participants motivated and enhances their learning experience.

Personalize and Tailor – Recognize that participants have varying levels of familiarity with your field. Provide options for both beginners and more advanced learners. Personalize the learning journey by offering different tracks or pathways.

Offer Practical Insights – Share practical insights that participants can apply directly to their endeavors. Real-life anecdotes, success stories, and challenges you've overcome can make your content relatable and actionable.

Facilitate Collaboration – Encourage participants to collaborate and interact with each other. This builds community and allows for knowledge-sharing among learners.

Provide Feedback – Offer constructive feedback on assignments or projects participants submit. This personalized guidance adds value and demonstrates your commitment to their growth.

Consider Various Formats – Explore different course formats, such as self-paced modules, live webinars, or hybrid models. This accommodates diverse learning preferences and schedules.

Leverage Technology – Utilize learning management systems (LMS), webinar platforms, and video hosting services to deliver your courses seamlessly and professionally.

Promote Your Offering – Use your existing online presence and networks to promote your training programs. Leverage social media, email marketing, and your website to reach your target audience.

Collect Feedback – Continuously seek feedback from participants to improve your courses. Their insights can help you refine content and enhance the learning experience.

Evolve and Expand – As you gain experience and gather feedback, consider expanding your course offerings. Develop advanced courses, workshops, or mentorship programs to cater to different learning levels.

Demonstrate Results – Showcase success stories of individuals who have benefited from your training. This demonstrates the tangible value participants can gain from your expertise.

Cultivate a Community – Beyond the course, create avenues for ongoing engagement, such as alumni networks or forums, where participants can continue learning and supporting each other.

Sharing your expertise through training and courses helps to give back to your industry, establishes you as a thought leader, and creates additional revenue streams. By following these steps and infusing your personal touch, you can create impactful learning experiences and help others to succeed in the results they are looking for.

Testimonials on Business Success

Let's talk about how customer testimonials can affect a business's success. A short while ago, I discussed how online training and coaching can connect with customers. Now, let's see how reviews and feedback can impact a business before we move on to creating customer relationships through "how to" content writing.

Customer testimonials are like happy stories from customers who really liked a business. These stories are important because they help people trust the business more, show that the business is respectable, and make new customers interested. When people hear about other people having good experiences, they start to feel surer about what the company offers.

These customer stories do the following things for a business:

Making Trust and Belief – Testimonials prove that a company is dependable. When new customers hear about good experiences, they're more likely to believe that the company is honest.

Helping People Decide to Buy – People trust other people's words more than advertisements. When people hear about good experiences from others, they're more likely to buy things, and they feel better about their decisions.

Making the Company Look Good – Happy stories from customers make a business seem better, which attracts both new customers and ones who already know about it.

Showing Real Proof – Testimonials are real stories that potential customers can understand and relate to, which helps them trust and like the brand.

Making Customer Relationships Stronger – When customers share their good experiences, it shows that they really like the company. When the company shares these stories, it makes the connection between the brand and customers stronger.

Standing Out from Others – Testimonials make a business different from its competitors. Stories from unique customers make the company seem better when compared to others.

Basically, customer testimonials are valuable for businesses. They help people decide to buy, make the company look good, show real stories, make customer relationships better, and help the business stand out. When a company uses these stories well, it shows possible customers that other people had good experiences, which makes them feel confident and trusting about choosing that company.

Creating How To Content in Your Niche

In businesses like food and drinks or other specialized areas, it's important to connect well with people. One way to do this is by sharing helpful and interesting "how to" guides. These guides show off your knowledge, encourage customers to try things themselves, build a community, and let people talk with you. This all leads to making special and memorable experiences for your customers. In this part, I'll talk about why sharing "how to" guides is so helpful to readers, and how to draft well written "how to" blog posts, which all fit into getting ready for teaching or doing a course. It all starts by giving your biggest fans a sneak peek at how things are done.

Giving Useful Information: People really like "how to" guides because they are given practical advice to solve specific problems or needs. When you share your knowledge, it makes your company a trusted source.

Encouraging Trying New Things: Through "how to" information, you can inspire site visitors to experiment with new stuff related to what you do. Whether it's exciting recipes for a food business or cool craft techniques for an artsy company, your guidance makes people want to learn new things.

Creating a community: Sharing "how to" guides bring together online visitors who love the same things you do. It makes them feel like they belong and are part of a group with shared interests, which makes them stick with your brand.

Letting People Talk Back: "How to" guides invited readers to correspond with your business. By letting them leave comments, feedback, and questions, you open a path for conversations.

Making Things Personal: When you adjust your "how to" to fit what your customers want and like, you're giving them a personal experience. This particularly makes customers happy with this personalized relationship.

Creating "How To" Blog Posts

To make good "how to" articles, consider the following:

Solving a Clear Problem – Start by saying the exact problem your article helps with. This makes sure your readers know what they're going to get.

Setting the Scene – Introduce your topic and make it interesting so readers want to keep going. This helps them see why the information you're sharing matters.

Step-by-Step Help – Break the process down into smaller parts that are easy to understand. Explain each step simply so anyone can follow along.

Using Pictures and Videos – Make your instructions clearer by adding good pictures and videos. These visuals help readers understand and do the steps right.

Sharing Tips and Warnings – Give extra help, warnings, and important info in your article. These things help readers avoid problems and make sure things turn out well.

Finishing Up – Summarize the steps and give any last thoughts or ideas. This reminds readers of the most important things in your article and leaves them feeling good.

Publishing "how to" guides relevant to your industry is an effective strategy to encourage repeat business from customers. By giving useful info, inspiring people to try new things, building a community, opening conversations, and making things personal, you build a strong link with your online researchers. Write your "how to" guides clearly, concisely, and in a way that's interesting. This way, your content really hits home with readers and helps them learn and spend more.

Thank you for reaching this point. At this stage, you're likely establishing a connection as you reach out to customers after each special event. Push yourself to apply these principles both in-person and online, even when you might not feel like it. is what sets apart those who persist with my system and those who just watch from the sidelines. Have faith in your abilities and your team to cultivate online relationships following pop-up shop activities. Speaking of activities, this leads me to introduce my upcoming Secret Guide, which will show you how to make your pop-up shop more efficient.

SECRET GUIDE #6: FOLLOW-UP AND BUILD RAPPORT

BUILD RAPPORT WORKSHEET – Make Lasting Impacts.

1. How does social media serve as a digital amphitheater, and what opportunities does it present for businesses in the context of pop-up events?

_____

_____

_____

_____

_____

2. How can blogging contribute to improving search engine rankings, according to the information provided?

_____

_____

_____

_____

_____

3. How can newsletters be utilized for promotions and discounts?

_____

_____

_____

_____

_____

SECRET GUIDE #7

Streamline Your Pop-up Shop for Success

Pop-up Transactions and Inventory Management Under One Portal.

Efficiency in Pop-up Shop Business

While navigating the world of temporary shop venues, I've learned that efficiency is key to finding success. On my journey as a "popupreneur," one important lesson stands out: the magic of simplicity. Whether it's organizing storage rooms, product development, or setting up the layout of pop-up shops, every step should be carefully thought through. In this guide, you will grasp the heart of basic operations to amplify productivity.

Think of tidying up a messy room. Just like arranging stuff in storage space, managing your inventory and labor is like putting everything in the right spot, making it easy to find things, capturing accurate data, and reducing confusion. This is where the foundation of an efficient pop-up shop begins. Uncover how to do the setup of your shop to make your operation run smoothly.

Setting up and displaying your shop significantly affects how customers feel. Imagine planning a route that guides shoppers through an interesting and easy shopping experience. Designing a well-thought-out layout has a big impact, making things clear and simple for customers. By smartly choosing and placing products while creating a welcoming atmosphere, you're not only making your shop look good but also making shopping easy.

The aim is to make things work better. Here I will use an example of a small business owner who sells natural fruit juices in various flavors. Let's imagine them doing the following: One of the first things they need to decide is how they want to serve their juices and what kind of experience they want to provide for customers.

They have two main options: setting up a juice fountain or bot-
tling the juices in advance before selling them.

The choice they make depends on what kind of experience they
want to create and their overall business strategy. If they want to
make things easy and efficient, especially for a temporary pop-up
shop, it might be better to go with bottled juices. This not only
simplifies the serving process but also caters to customers who
prefer to grab a bottle and go rather than wait in line for a freshly
poured cup.

It's important to note that this bottled approach might work best
for a temporary pop-up shop, not necessarily a permanent store.
Why? Well, with a pop-up shop, it's easier to move from place
to place without dealing with heavy equipment like drink fountains. Setting up and maintaining those fountains can be time-
consuming and may require strict hygiene standards at different
events. Plus, it could mean needing more staff to serve quickly,
which might increase labor costs.

This is a basic example of a smart change that can make a business run more smoothly and improve the customer experience,
especially in a temporary setting. And this idea of simplifying operations without compromising the customer experience can apply to other products as well.

For instance, think about a bakery that sells freshly baked artisanal bread. They face a similar choice of how to present their
bread to customers, whether it's pre-packaged or sliced on demand. Each option has its pros and cons, depending on what
kind of experience the bakery owner wants to offer and how efficiently they want to run their pop-up bakery. Once again, when
I say think simple, it's important to understand that an

entrepreneur with a clear vision may choose to use a strategy that
seems complicated and not very effective to others at first.

I hope this example has sparked some ideas as you plan what to
sell from your online store and how to present it in a way that's
easy for both you and your shoppers. As we go further into the
topic of efficiency, choosing what you sell and how you sell is a
topic worth mentioning. When you bring together your most
popular items, presented with ease, you're not only making your
inventory less complicated but also ensuring your pop-up shop
has what customers want most, hassle-free. This goes perfectly
with the idea of streamlining your POS system as well—achieving great results while keeping things simple.

Integrated POS

Streamlining isn't just about tangible stuff or merchandise that
you carry; it also includes technology. Having a strong point-of-
sale system (POS) that handles inventory, sales tracking, and employee monitoring makes things a lot easier while you grow your
business. These systems collect important data, giving you insights that help you make decisions. With a well-integrated POS,
in-person and online sales blend seamlessly, giving a full view of
how your company is doing. These systems aren't just add-ons;
they are a central part of the whole streamlined approach.

In a pop-up shop business, being quick and efficient is required.
The combination of technology and convenience facilitates a
winning operational flow. This leads me to share with you a
few game-changing point-of-sale systems—ones that don't just
handle sales in real time but also bring together inventory management in a simple, easy-to-use portal. These technologies

empower pop-up shop businesses, taking their operations to a whole new level of efficiency.

So, let's dance between technology, consumers, and business, where the art of streamlining transforms your shop into a model of efficiency. You will learn of tools and ideas that will confidently propel your online retail venture into the future of pop-up shops. Let's get started!

POS for Better Results

Making things run smoother – When a business streamlines its POS, it's like clearing out a cluttered, unorganized area. This helps the business work more efficiently by making transactions quicker and easier. This means shorter lines, less waiting, and fewer mistakes. All of this leads to customers being happier.

Spending Less Money – Imagine if a magic wand could make parts of a business's money-handling process automatic. This would save a lot of money by cutting down on how much people need to do things by hand. When things are automated, it avoids errors that can make money disappear.

Managing Items for Sale Better – A streamlined POS helps to keep a better eye on what you're selling. It's like having a bird's eye view of what's flying off the shelves and what's still sitting there. This helps in managing inventory well, not wasting anything, and making sure customers always find what they want.

Making More Sales – Think about a shop where you can pay in many ways, things get scanned super-fast, and the staff always seem to know what you need. This kind of smooth experience makes customers want to come back more often. They might

even tell their friends. That's what a streamlined system can help
do.

Keeping Things Safe – A well-constructed POS also acts like a su-
perhero shield for businesses. It helps in stopping bad guys who
might want to steal information. By having this shield, or in technological terms, firewall, you show customers that your company's technology is safe and you can be trusted with their info and
money.

In a nutshell, making the POS simpler helps your company perform better in many ways: they work better, don't spend too
much, sell more, and stay safe. This all comes together to make
the business stronger and able to keep going for a long time.

Having a system that simplifies the point-of-sale process using
the likes of Square or Clover is like connecting riddle pieces. This
riddle includes your e-commerce store, your physical storefront,
and temporary pop-up shops. When all these pieces fit together,
it's a win-win situation for you and your customers.

Now that you have seen some benefits of a well-functioning
POS, let's take a glimpse at what lies ahead. In the upcoming
sections, I will guide you through the process of using streamlined POS, whether it's Square, Clover, or similar options like
Wix. You will see how to mix your online store information with
what's happening in your temporary shops. Plus, I will talk about
why it's so important to keep everything in one system. It's like
having all your tools in one toolbox, ready to fix anything that
comes your way.

Pop-up Shop POS with E-commerce

Let me start off by saying it's best practice to link the system that tracks your in-store and pop-up sales with the data on your online shop. As an increasing number of businesses transition to the digital space, customers seek a seamless and consistent experience across all their interactions with your brand. This implies that the information they receive when they visit your physical storefront if you own one and a temporary shop, should support what they see on your website. This encompasses details like product availability and pricing. Nevertheless, there are instances where disparities might arise, particularly if you offer limited items exclusive to specific locations or if prices vary due to factors like shipping costs included in the online final price. If these situations apply, transparently communicate these aspects to customers engaging in both online and offline shopping.

By integrating your sales tracking system with your online store, you ensure the accuracy of inventory information, regardless of where a customer chooses to shop. This diminishes the risk of inadvertently overselling items beyond your actual stock, preventing disappointed customers and the need to cancel orders. Moreover, this integration provides you with a clearer understanding of the quantity of each product in stock, enabling informed decisions when replenishing your inventory.

Furthermore, the synchronization of your sales tracking system and online store yields valuable insights into your clientele. This data proves invaluable for tailoring marketing campaigns to specific customer segments and elevates their overall shopping experience.

Maximizing Efficiency

Square and Clover are two popular POS that offer robust features for businesses of all sizes. These systems allow you to track revenue, labor, and inventory across all your operations, including e-commerce, brick and mortar, and pop-up shops.

One of the most significant benefits of using a system like the ones mentioned here is the ability to access real-time data across all operations. This means that you can track your revenue, labor costs, and inventory levels in real time.

These systems also offer enhanced reporting features, allowing you to generate detailed reports on your business's performance. These reports can be used to identify trends and opportunities for growth, as well as to identify areas where you may need to make improvements.

Online Store and Pop-up Shop's POS

Pop-up shops undoubtedly help to reach new customers and expand the business's reach. However, managing inventory and sales data for these temporary shops can be challenging, especially if you are using a separate POS system.

POS included in your pop-up shop operations allows you to track sales and inventory in real time, meaning easy transfer of products between locations and ensuring that your inventory levels are accurate across all channels.

Additionally, integrating your online payment system with your pop-up shop allows a seamless checkout experience for your customers. They then can pay using their preferred method, whether it's cash, credit, or mobile payments.

Connecting your online store with a modern POS is a worthwhile investment. This integration streamlines your operations, making it easier to manage everything in one place. It benefits both you as a business owner and your customers, resulting in improved efficiency, and profitability.

When you merge your POS with your e-commerce website, your product inventory remains accurate across all platforms. Plus, you can gather customer data, which helps you make smarter purchasing decisions. Streamlining means you gain access to advanced reporting features. These features allow you to create detailed reports and spot opportunities for growth.

Initiate Website Transactions

When it comes to starting transactions on a website builder, the process can be seen as the digital doorway to your business. Imagine it as the elegant passage connecting you and your potential customers, creating a smooth and effortless path for them to engage with your products or services. Here, I'll discuss a variety of ways you can kickstart these interactions, ensuring that your diverse array of customers can easily find what they need and make purchases with utmost convenience.

Pre-Ordering for Pop-Up Shop Pickups – Think of this as the virtual queue that lets your customers reserve their spot in line. It's like reserving a table at a restaurant, but in this case, it's securing their spot for a special event or pop-up shop experience. With a few clicks, your customers can pre-order items they want to pick up at your pop-up venues. This helps you anticipate demand and creates a sense of exclusivity and anticipation.

Pre-Ordering for Curbside Pickup – Imagine the convenience of curbside pickup—just like when you grab your favorite coffee without leaving your car. Now, translate that into your online store. Customers can pre-order items and specify when they'll swing by to collect them, creating a super-efficient and contactless shopping experience. This is like having your own personal shopper, except you're both the shopkeeper and the shopper!

Order Placement for USPS/FedEx (Courier) Delivery – Visualize this as a virtual postman, delivering happiness right to your customers' doorsteps. With this method, customers can place orders for items they want to be shipped to them. It's as easy as selecting items, entering an address, and voila—your carefully packaged products are on the way, spreading joy and excitement. This option transcends distances, connecting you with customers far and wide.

Personalized Local Delivery – Imagine the friendly neighborhood store owner who knows your name and exactly where you live. Apply this warmth to the digital realm. Customers within a certain radius can enjoy the luxury of having their orders hand-delivered to their doorstep. It's like having a local market that comes to you. This saves them time and promotes a sense of community

Inventory Management and Sales Tracking – Envision an astute assistant who keeps an eagle eye on your products. This feature is akin to a digital manager that tracks your inventory levels and monitors sales trends. It ensures you never run out of stock unexpectedly and offers insights into which items are flying off the virtual shelves. This way, you're always one step ahead.

In essence, the process of initiating transactions on a website is like orchestrating a symphony of convenience, diversity, and efficiency. It's about providing your customers with a rich menu of options, allowing them to engage with your business in ways that best suit their needs. Whether they're eagerly awaiting a pop-up shop, seeking contactless curbside pickup, embracing the thrill of online orders, enjoying the personal touch of local delivery, or benefiting from meticulous inventory management, your e-commerce website serves as the gateway to an unparalleled shopping experience.

Third-Party Shipping Services

Third-party shipping services are companies that specialize in helping businesses manage their shipping needs. These services can tie in with websites and Point of Sale systems (POS) to streamline the shipping process. Let's take a closer look at some types of third-party shipping services that can be integrated with website builders and POS:

Pirate Ship – Pirate Ship is a popular third-party shipping service that offers cost-effective shipping solutions for businesses. It integrates well with e-commerce websites and POS. It provides a user-friendly interface where you can import orders, compare shipping rates from various carriers (like USPS, FedEx, and UPS), and generate shipping labels. Pirate Ship is known for its simplicity and ability to provide discounted shipping rates, making it a great choice for small to medium-sized businesses.

Shippo – Shippo is another versatile shipping service that plugs in well with websites and POS. It offers a unified platform to connect with multiple carriers, allowing businesses to compare rates, generate labels, and track shipments. Shippo's integration

capabilities make it easy for businesses to automate shipping processes and provide real-time tracking information to customers.

Ship Station – Ship Station is a comprehensive shipping platform
that connects with e-commerce websites and POS. It supports
integration with a wide range of marketplaces and shopping
carts. Ship Station offers features like batch processing, custom-
branded packing slips, and order management. It enables businesses to efficiently process orders, print labels, and manage
shipments.

Easy Ship – Easy Ship is a global shipping platform that special-
izes in cross-border e-commerce. It connects with various carriers worldwide, helping businesses calculate accurate shipping
costs, manage customs documentation, and provide international shipping options to customers. Easy ship integration with
websites and POS ensures a smooth shipping experience for
both domestic and international orders.

Shipping Easy – Shipping Easy is designed to simplify shipping for
e-commerce businesses. It integrates with popular shopping
carts and marketplaces to centralize order processing. Businesses
can compare shipping rates, print labels, and automated tracking
notifications. Shipping Easy also offers inventory management
features, making it a valuable tool for businesses looking to
streamline their operations.

Ordoro – Ordoro is a shipping and inventory management that
works well with websites and POS. It enables businesses to manage orders, track inventory levels, and print shipping labels.
Ordoro's integration features help businesses efficiently handle
their order fulfillment process and maintain accurate inventory
records.

These third-party services provide businesses with tools to optimize their shipping operations, enhance customer satisfaction, and save on shipping costs. Their helpful features can allow your business to focus on growing the brand while leaving the complexities of shipping logistics to them, the experts.

Reputable POS Systems

There are many different Point of Sale Systems available that businesses use to handle their sales process. These systems come with various features, abilities, and costs. Here are some of the best systems possibly suited for your pop-up shop:

Square POS – Square is a well-liked system that offers a wide range of tools for businesses, regardless of their size. It provides ways to handle transactions, keep track of inventory, and store customer information. You can even accept payments through mobile devices and connect with online selling. Square also provides a free mobile app and reasonably priced equipment for businesses that want to save money.

Lightspeed Retail – Lightspeed Retail operates using the cloud and is designed especially for retail businesses. It comes with functions to manage your inventory, oversee employees, and keep track of customer relationships. You can also access reports and analysis tools. Lightspeed Retail can even link up with e-commerce platforms and other external applications.

Shopify POS – Shopify is popular for online selling and has POS for physical and temporary storefronts. You can handle transactions, manage your inventory, and store customer details using this system. It also lets you connect with your online store.

Shopify POS offers reasonably priced equipment and a user-friendly interface that's easy to understand.

Toast POS – Toast is also cloud-based and popularly created for restaurants. It assists with things like managing menus, taking orders at the table, and overseeing kitchen operations. You can even set up online orders and deliveries. Toast POS provides tools to generate reports and analyze data, which helps restaurants make their operations more efficient.

Vend POS – Vend is cloud-based and tailored for retail businesses. It comes with features for handling inventory, managing customers, and producing reports. You can also link it to your online store. Vend provides a variety of equipment options and an interface that's easy to use.

Clover POS – Clover is designed for smaller to medium-sized businesses. It helps with processing transactions, keeping track of inventory, and managing customer information. You can also connect it with external applications. Clover offers different equipment options and a user-friendly interface.

ShopKeep – Recognized as the top choice for food trucks, offering a robust POS system tailored to the needs of mobile food businesses.

eHopper – Known for affordability without compromising on features, making it an ideal choice for pop-up shops seeking a comprehensive POS solution.

Revel – Considered the best iPad-based POS system, offering advanced features and functionalities for pop-up shops.

These are just a few examples of systems available for businesses. When choosing a POS system, it's important to consider what you specifically need, how much you can afford, and the features each system offers.

Now that you are familiar with some of the top POS available, let's shift our focus to a specific scenario that often presents a unique challenge: operating offline at pop-up shop venues where there is no internet connection or Wi-Fi available. In such situations, ensure that you choose a system that's equipped to handle transactions, manage inventory, and perform other essential functions without relying on an internet connection. This requires careful consideration of the offline capabilities and features offered by these systems. Read on and see how some of these, if so, can adapt to such offline environments and continue to serve your business without internet connectivity. With that being said, do your due diligence and research which ones have the offline capability. The one I have used in the past with that functionality is Square.

Operating Offline (No Internet Connection or Wi-Fi)

It's important for Point of Sales to perform transactions offline because it ensures that business operations can continue even if there is a disruption to the network connection or if the internet is down. There are a few reasons why this is important:

Network Instability – In some areas, network connections may not be reliable, and in these circumstances, an offline mode can help ensure that transactions can still be processed. This is especially important for pop-up companies that operate in areas with unreliable network connectivity.

Internet Outages – Even if the network is generally reliable, there may be instances where the internet goes down. An offline mode can ensure that transactions can still be processed and customers can still make purchases.

Increased Security – An offline mode can also increase security because it reduces the risk of data breaches and hacking. When a POS operates offline, there is no risk of data being intercepted during transmission over a network, which can be a vulnerability in online transactions.

Overall, an offline mode for a POS system is an important feature to ensure business continuity and security, even in the face of network or internet disruptions.

Being involved with the world of pop-ups has really highlighted how crucial efficiency is for success. Over the course of more than five years of operating a pop-up shop, excluding the times spent working alongside my two wizapreneurs, I've strived for simplicity in all facets of the business, from establishing the physical layout to integrating technology. Dealing with the complexities of transactions and managing inventory in pop-ups made it clear that having a strong point-of-sale system (POS) is key to making things run smoothly—it's something you really need to embrace.

Integrating POS systems isn't just a nice extra; it's a central part of how to make pop-up shop processes more efficient.

Now, let's talk about the next point, titled "Assign Online Duties to Sales Team: Set E-commerce Permissions for the Members of Your Salesforce." We're shifting from the physical world of pop-up shops to the digital side, where the connection between technology, consumers, and business gets a bit more complicated. We'll look at how to blend online and offline approaches for a well-rounded strategy.

I have addressed the enhancement of pop-up shop operations in this topic, covering everything from establishing the physical space to the use of technology through streamlining. Moving forward, we'll focus on giving the sales team online responsibilities and explore the details of setting e-commerce permissions for Salesforce members. The story will keep unfolding, guiding you through the changing pop-up marketplace and stressing the importance of being efficient and adaptable for lasting success.

STREAMLINE POP-UP SHOP WORKSHEET –
Aim to Maximize Productivity.

1. How does the setup and display of a shop affect customer experience?

_____

_____

_____

_____

_____

2. What factors should be considered when choosing a POS system for a pop-up shop?

_____

_____

_____

_____

_____

SECRET GUIDE #8

Assign Online Duties to Sales Team

Set E-commerce Permissions for the Members of your Salesforce.

Y ou have once again stumbled upon a very helpful part of my framework. The following guide will help you stay ahead while you grow and scale your shop. I've got some more exciting ideas to share that have been working for my business since discovering how to pop-up an e-commerce business.

Here in this secret, I will start off by discussing cross-training relating to the online duties and responsibilities of your team members.

Cross-Training

Let's talk about how cross-training your salesforce can seriously boost your online operation, especially when it comes to using pop-up shops.

So, here's the deal: the first step in this process is to do your best to build an outstanding sales team. I'm talking about folks who not only know how to sell on purpose like pros but also really understand what your company is all about.

As we move along, tackling everything from bridging the gap between offline and online, building strong customer relationships, and boosting team collaboration helps to keep up with the ever-changing business scene. The steps I have outlined here will create a team that exceeds the challenges of today's market.

Think of this guide as a GPS for the entire process. In the upcoming steps, I'll break down simple and easy-to-follow actions, explaining why cross-training, adaptability, and sharing a common vision are crucial. The goal is to help you create a sales team that's on the same page, driving your business straight to success.

Step 1: Getting Started with Building a Strong Sales Team – To make this all work, the first step is to build a team that knows how to handle your pop-up shop operations. Before diving into the digital world, your salespeople need to understand your company's overall purpose and goals. This means more than just knowing how to sell—they need to be on board with your vision and approach.

Step 2: The Challenge of Bridging Offline and Online – Transitioning from online to physical requires an adaptable salesforce. Imagine having your sales team not only sell products in person but also write blogs, manage social media, handle data, and support customers online. This diverse skill set makes your team incredibly versatile and ready to help your business in many ways.

Step 3: Boosting Customer Relations and Loyalty – When your sales team truly grasps your company's vision, they can explain the real value of your products and services to customers. This leads to more personalized interactions that make customers feel like a person and not a slot machine. They also feel valued and understood. And as we all know, happy customers tend to stick around and spread the word.

Step 4: Better Team Collaboration and Communication – Cross-training encourages better communication between different parts of your company. When your salespeople understand the big picture, they can work effectively with other teams as you expand your enterprise, like marketing and customer support. This teamwork ensures everyone's on the same page, making your business run smoother. In case you are not planning on expanding anytime soon, your sales members will assume the roles of marketing and customer support.

Step 5: Adapting and Thriving – Having a team with a range of skills means they can easily switch between projects and tasks. This flexibility is super handy, even if you're running a small business without separate departments. It keeps everything running like a well-oiled machine.

Step 6: Tailoring the Sales Approach – When your salespeople really understand what your customers need are, they can tailor their sales pitches accordingly. This leads to better sales results, as they can meet customers' exact requirements.

Step 7: Everyone Pulling in the Same Direction – Cross-training helps your team see how their individual roles fit into the bigger picture. This shared understanding creates a sense of unity and purpose, leading to more teamwork, better productivity, and overall success.

Cross-training your sales team might sound like a bit of extra work, but trust me, the benefits are worth the effort. From better teamwork to more adaptability, there's a lot to gain. With a team that's skilled in various areas, your business will thrive, especially in the world of pop-up shops connecting with the world of the digital network.

So, if you're looking to level up your e-commerce game, consider cross-training your salespeople. They'll become your secret weapon for growth, happy customers, and a thriving business.

Cross Training Positions

Diversifying the skill sets of your sales team can greatly benefit your e-commerce business. Hence, I have outlined seven specialties of sales representatives who can be trained to handle different roles within the company's online operations. Now here are some of the likely cross positions to understand for the success of your "*Popup Your E-commerce*" business.

Blog Writing – When sales reps are trained in blog writing, they become proficient content creators. By sharing their knowledge, insights, and familiarity with products through blog posts, they establish themselves as experts in your industry. This type of engaging and informative content attracts potential customers and builds trust. Their understanding of customers from the grassroots level enables them to craft compelling content that connects with the target audience.

Social Media Sharing – Social media is a powerful tool for brand promotion, and customer interaction is needed in this instance. Training your sales team in social media usage empowers them to effectively utilize these social networks to increase brand visibility and engage with customers.

Sales reps can curate and share relevant content, respond to customer queries, and actively participate in discussions related to your products and industry topics. By applying social media skills, they contribute strongly to your online marketing efforts.

Data Entry – Accurate and up-to-date data is crucial for informed decision-making and smooth business operations. Training your sales team in data entry certifies they can maintain and update databases, manage customer information (like email lists), and track sales metrics. This frees up your time from routine tasks and equips them with insights into customer likings, buying patterns, and market trends. Prepared with this knowledge, they can adjust their strategies to optimize sales opportunities.

Online Customer Support (Email, Live Chat, Correspondence) – Exceptional customer support is vital for e-commerce success. Training your team in online customer support enhances the customer experience and boosts satisfaction. Sales reps can handle inquiries, provide product details, solve issues, and address concerns through channels like email, live chat, and correspondence.

This seamless integration of sales and support guarantees swift and effective customer service, leading to improved customer loyalty and repeat business.

By cross-training your sales team in these online roles, you tap into the varied talents of your staff. This multi-skilled employment maximizes resource utilization and cultivates a nimble and adaptable workforce. Sales leaders become well-rounded professionals capable of contributing to different facets of the business, driving growth and achievement.

Moreover, this cross-training initiative encourages personal and professional development. As employees gain new skills and expand their knowledge, they feel empowered and motivated, resulting in greater job satisfaction and employee retention.

The enriched skill set also opens pathways for career advancement within the organization, as employees can take on more diverse and challenging roles as your company expands.

By training in online positions like blog writing, social media sharing, data entry, and online customer support, you create a versatile and capable workforce. This maximizes the potential of each team member, enabling them to contribute to various business facets and align their skills with the evolving demands of the e-commerce industry and pop-up shop procedures. Consequently, your company gains a competitive edge, delivers outstanding customer experiences, and positions itself for long-term success.

Customer Relationship Management (CRM)

We've explored how a well-trained sales team can boost your online business's success. Empowering your staff with versatile skills offers significant advantages. Another part of growth and building lasting customer relationships involves Customer Relationship Management (CRM). A strong CRM strategy supports your adaptable sales team, helping you connect better with customers, make informed choices, and improve your business operations. Let's delve into CRM and learn how it can elevate your online venture.

The Pros and Cons of Employee CRM Access – CRM systems play a key role in managing customer interactions and driving business growth. Deciding whether to give employees access to your website's CRM system is an important decision to make. This decision comes with both benefits and risks. In this section, we'll explore the potential advantages and challenges of granting employees CRM access and its impact on collaboration, customer service, data accuracy, and security.

Benefits of Employee CRM Access

Better Collaboration – By letting employees access the CRM, you encourage teamwork and communication. With shared customer information, your team can collaborate effectively, leading to improved problem-solving and team effort.

Improved Customer Service – Employee CRM access provides insights into customer interactions, allowing personalized assistance and better recommendations. This leads to higher customer satisfaction.

Accurate Data – Employee access keeps customer information up to date. Maintaining quality data helps with informed choices, dependable reports, and information for growth.

Risks of Employee CRM Access

Data Security – Allowing access raises security concerns. Robust security measures like authentication and encryption are crucial to protect customer data. Employee training in data security is vital, too.

Improper Data Use – Access to sensitive data poses the risk of misuse. Educating employees on confidentiality and privacy, along with clear policies, minimizes data mishandling.

System Strain – Too many users can strain the system's performance. Managing user access and permissions ensures a smooth experience.

Giving your sales team access to CRM tools offers benefits to your e-commerce businesses. But it's important to address risks like data breaches and system strain.

Implement strong security, educate employees, and manage access carefully. With proper policies, employee CRM access becomes an asset for customer-focused strategies and overall website growth.

Connections with Teams and Customers

Have you ever thought about showing your team members' profiles on your website? It's a way to let your customers know who's behind the scenes and what they're responsible for. For example, Warehouse Clerk. This can make your business more open and connected. Not only does it give your website a personal touch, but it also builds trust and a better relationship with your audience. Let's find out how this can make your online business even better.

So why put your team's profile information on your website? Here are some good reasons:

Builds Trust – When people visit your site, they want to know who they're dealing with. Sharing your team's photos and details helps customers feel more comfortable and friendly toward your company.

Shows Expertise – Sharing your team's info lets you show off their skills and experience. This proves that your team is talented and knowledgeable.

Increases Credibility – When customers can see other real people, other than your pop-up sales team, behind your company, it makes your business deemed more credible. It also gives customers a better sense of your values and dedication to quality.

Furthers Connection – Sharing your team's profiles helps customers feel like they know your company better. Learning about personalities beyond interaction at venues can create a stronger bond between your organization and patrons.

Recruitment – Having your team's information on your site can also attract new employees. When potential hires can learn about your team and company culture, they might be more interested in joining.

Overall, team profiles placed on your website can be extremely beneficial. It builds trust, shows expertise, makes you more credible, helps you connect with customers, and even attracts new team members. Plus, it makes your company stand out and offers visitors a more personal and interesting experience.

To make your pop-up shop successful, it's not just about having a good sales team. You also need to train them to handle various tasks online. Connecting what happens offline and online is important for better teamwork. Each step in this process helps create a team that can adapt, thrive, and work together well.

Now, if you have been using the tips from Secret Guides 1 to 8 for your online and e-commerce business, the next secret is to keep an eye on how well you're doing.

Get to know analytic tools that help you analyze data and see how you are performing online. This will give you a better idea of how your efforts have been so far.

ASSIGN ONLINE DUTIES WORKSHEET – Inspire Your Team.

1. How does cross-training contribute to making a sales team adaptable, especially in bridging offline and online operations?

_____

_____
_____
_____
_____

2. How does cross-training maximize resource utilization and contribute to a nimble and adaptable workforce?

_____

_____
_____
_____
_____

3. Name and briefly explain two positions mentioned in the guide that sales representatives can be trained for in addition to their sales roles.

_____

_____
_____
_____
_____

SECRET GUIDE #9
Track and Analyze Your Efforts

Familiarize with Analytic Tools and Measure Performance.

Welcome to an important place of our journey: "Track and Analyze Your Efforts." In this secret, you will notice something that's often forgotten when you are too busy running your day-to-day operation. Imagine it like finding a hidden path in a maze—it might be easy to miss, but once you see it, it can change everything.

Think about all the things you must do when you run an online store and set up pop-up shops. There are many tasks, right? Well, what I'm about to share is like having a secret map that shows you what's working and what's not. I've talked about exciting stuff so far—like running pop-up shops and learning about this remarkable business framework—but now, it's time to take a step back.

So, you've been experimenting with what I've suggested. Maybe you've set up pop-up venues, learned about and acted on some of the strategies, and also used a handful of digital marketing tools. That's fantastic! But here's the thing—before you keep charging ahead, it's a good idea to stop and look at what you've done. Ask yourself questions like: Am I doing what Damian said in the right way? Is it making a difference? And how do I know if it's working or not?

Imagine you're baking a cake. You wouldn't just put everything together and hope for the best, right? You'd check if it's cooking properly and if it's rising like it should. It's the same here. You need to see if your efforts are creating the results you want.

Now, if you're already taking a closer look at your work, that's awesome! But if you haven't really started, I've got a piece of advice: become someone who uses data to make decisions and further actions, even if it seems a bit complicated.

Remember, I've said before none of the to-dos in this book happen by accident. Everything I recommend is deliberate, including analyzing data to understand your business's current state and anticipate future developments.

Data is like having special magnifying glasses that let you see more clearly. Sometimes, you'll need to dig deep to find answers, like when you're trying to solve a puzzle. Other times, you'll see the results right away, like when you try a recipe and it comes out perfectly. For instance, if you've been using pop-up shops to boost your online storefront, you might notice that certain actions lead to more people buying things online. Agree? But wait, there's a twist.

Let's say you set up a special landing page for a popular product, and several people start ordering it online. You might think it's because the page is optimized so magnificently, which might be the case. But what if I told you that some of those buyers saw the product at your pop-up shop, then visited your website and made a purchase? It's like a detective story—figuring out where the results are coming from.

And guess what? There are tools for that—tools that help to analyze the clues and make sense of the story. Here's another example: let's say you're telling people at your pop-up shop to buy from your website and also leave a Google review. But as time passes, you notice that while people are buying, the Google reviews aren't coming in. This is where tracking comes in handy.

All it takes is a simple change, like adding a pop-up venue QR code that goes directly to Google Business Profile to initiate reviews. These QR codes will lead people directly to where they can leave a review. It's like giving customers a shortcut, making it easy for them to leave feedback while everything is fresh in their minds. Suddenly, you're not just guessing – you're using what you know to make improvements.

The goal is to understand where your visitors are coming from, what they do on your site, and where they go next. Are they coming directly from your pop-up shop events? Did they find you on social media? Is your website getting lots of visitors because of your amazing, well-optimized blog posts? It's like decoding a mystery. And when you solve it, you make your business better with these fresh perspectives.

So, dear popupreneurs, this is the magic of tracking and analyzing. It's like having special tools that help you see things clearly. Every action you take, every step you follow—they all leave clues. And with the right tools, you can uncover those clues and use them to guide your business journey. Let's dive in together and look at the tools that might change the way you see your business—they might not all be the latest, but they're like a treasure chest for anyone trying to navigate the world of business with data.

Begin with Search Engine Tools.

Your aim should always be to improve your online presence and connect with the people you want to reach. Thankfully, search engines like Google, Bing, and Yahoo have some incredibly useful tools that can really make a difference. These tools— think Google Analytics, Bing Webmaster Tools, Yahoo Analytics, and more—aren't just for SEO experts. They're like your secret helpers in the online world. They can help your business grow and shine across various search engines.

One major advantage of using them is that they let you peek into your site performance. You can find out how many people are visiting your site, what they're doing there, and how many of them are making purchases. This information gives you a clear view of what's going well and what might need to be addressed. You can know the number of visitors you're getting, see which pages they're loving the most, and understand how frequently they're hitting that "buy" button. Armed with this insight, you can make thoughtful conclusions to level up your e-commerce business.

There's more—these analytical tools also shed light on how people are using your site, not just visiting it. You can see how they stumbled upon your site pages, and even what topics pique their interest the most. It's a bit like studying a map of where your customers are wandering.

By analyzing the data, you decipher what they're into and what they're searching for. Equipped with this data, you can enhance your website pages and give potential site visitors exactly what they're searching on SERP.

But wait, this is where the details get even more exciting! These search engine tools can reveal precisely where your customers are coming from. And I deem this very important! Did they find you through a link someone shared? It's like knowing which paths lead to your online shop. You can see the routes people are taking to discover landing pages. Maybe they're arriving through a search engine's (SERP) organic results, or perhaps they're tapping links on social media. This helps to channel your efforts wisely and further attract more visitors.

And that's not all—these tools bring forth insights into your sales, your target audience, and even your competition. This information lets you see what's trending, what items are popular, and how you're stacking up against your rivals. This knowledge surely will empower you as an e-commerce business owner. It did for me.

And here's something awesome for local businesses, especially those running pop-up shops. There are more tools that ensure your business gets spotted when people search for a topic of interest nearby—like what you're selling. Think about platforms such as Google Business Profile, Bing Places for Business, and Yahoo Small Business. They let you create a profile that shares details about your location, opening hours, and the services you provide. When someone searches for something related to your business in your area, your company will show it in their local SERP. This really helps you connect with local customers.

Without further ado, here is a list of Google tools that you must become familiar with, and I recommend you use them if you are not already.

Google

As an e-commerce entrepreneur who also engages in pop-up storefront operations, you're constantly seeking ways to enhance your online authority and drive growth. Luckily, this selection of analytics can greatly assist you in achieving these goals. While Google Analytics, Google Search Console, and Google Business Profile are essential, there are also others like Moz, SEMrush, Ahrefs, and many more that can prove invaluable to your progress. Those I will go over later in this section.

But first I will briefly define some of Google's owned tools and how they can help you make data-driven decisions and propel your online growth efforts.

Google Analytics – Google Analytics is a cornerstone tool that allows you to measure and understand your website's performance. With comprehensive insights into traffic, user behavior, and conversion rates, you evaluate how well your website is performing and identify areas for improvement. By tracking the number of visitors, analyzing user engagement on specific pages, and measuring conversion rates, you gain valuable data that offers possible solutions.

Google Search Console – Google Search Console is one of my favorite tools to use. They assist in improving your online visibility and search engine optimization (SEO) efforts. It provides information about how Google crawls and indexes your website, enabling you to monitor and boost your site's performance in search rankings. By leveraging the insights provided by Google Search Console, you identify potential issues that may be hindering your website's visibility and analyze the keywords driving organic traffic to your site. This knowledge allows you to optimize your content and take strategic measures to improve your search engine rankings.

Google Business Profile – This can be suitable for e-commerce or online business entrepreneurs with a pop-up shop that operates pure e-commerce. It is also for a retail storefront or if you operate out of a commercialized building of some sort. Google Business Profile is an indispensable platform for strengthening your local visibility and connecting with your target audience. By creating a Google Business Profile listing, you provide information such as your address, contact details, business hours, and customer reviews. This ensures that when potential customers search for relevant products or services in your locality, your business's listing appears prominently in search results, increasing the likelihood of attracting your local community.

Although not discussed in detail here, there are other search engines, such as Bing and Yahoo, with analytics tools that you can also use to help with your online exposure. They work pretty much the same way.

Non-Google Tools

Moz – Moz uncovers SEO opportunities and analyzes competitors. Moz is a comprehensive SEO tool that offers a range of features to optimize your website's performance. It provides insights into keyword rankings, backlink profiles, and site health, so you to uncover opportunities and identify areas where you can improve. Additionally, Moz's competitive analysis features enable you to analyze your competitors' strategies and stay one step ahead in the market.

SEMrush – SEMrush is another powerful analytics tool that can help you drive traffic and refine your marketing strategies. As previously discussed in Secret Guide #2, SEMrush offers features like keyword research, competitive analysis, and PPC (pay-per-click) advertising insights. With SEMrush, you can identify high-value keywords, know your competitors' tactics, and optimize your PPC campaigns to attract targeted traffic to your e-commerce store.

Ahrefs – This tool offers a comprehensive SEO toolset mentioned in the earlier sections of this book that focuses on backlink analysis and competitive research. It allows you to analyze your website's backlink profile, identify internal link-building opportunities, and monitor your competitors' backlinks. By leveraging Ahrefs, you can improve your SEO plan, enhance your website's authority, and ultimately increase your organic search visibility.

Hootsuite – Hootsuite is a social media management platform that helps businesses manage their online presence across multiple social media channels, including Facebook, Twitter, LinkedIn, Instagram, and others. The platform provides a centralized dashboard for managing social media activity, allowing users to schedule and publish posts, monitor mentions and messages, track engagement, and measure the impact of their social media efforts. Hootsuite also offers analytics and reporting tools to help users understand the performance of their social media campaigns and identify areas for improvement. The platform also integrates with a range of other marketing tools, including marketing automation, email marketing, and analytics platforms, to provide a solution for managing social media and other digital marketing activities.

These tools are a must-know or familiarization for e-commerce entrepreneurs who wish to make data-driven decisions, optimize their online presence, and drive growth. By owning the power of Google Analytics, Google Search Console, and Google Business Profile, as well as utilizing additional tools like Moz, SEMrush, and Ahrefs, you get a closer look into your website's performance, improve your SEO efforts, refine your marketing, and ultimately achieve success in e-commerce.

Built-in Analytics

Website builders offer a variety of built-in analytic tools that allow e-commerce site owners to track and analyze important metrics related to their site's performance. These are just examples of a few; there are many more, and new ones are continuously emerging. Coming up is a short list of some popular website builders you can try and their respective analytic tools.

There are many more, and the ones I am covering here are not necessarily the best, just four of the many options. Plus, some of the information that I have provided about these website builder analytics tools is available in the public domain. If you choose or convert to any on my list or decide to go with something else, please do further research.

Wix – Wix provides a built-in analytics dashboard called Wix Analytics. It offers detailed insights into visitor behavior, traffic sources, page views, and more. Users can monitor their site's performance, track conversion rates, and understand audience demographics. The tool also includes e-commerce analytics for online stores, helping track sales and revenue.

Squarespace – Squarespace offers Squarespace Analytics, which provides a overview of website traffic, popular content, referral sources, and visitor behavior. Users can access real-time data, set up conversion funnels, and gain insights into their audience. Like most website builders, Squarespace Analytics also integrates with popular third-party tools like Google Analytics.

Weebly – Weebly's built-in analytics offers an easy-to-use interface for tracking website performance. Users can monitor visitor statistics, traffic sources, and popular pages. It also provides e-commerce analytics, allowing online store owners to track sales, conversion rates, and customer behavior.

WordPress – WordPress also provides built-in analytics through its Jetpack plugin. Jetpack Analytics offers detailed insight into site traffic, search engine terms, and visitor behavior. It allows users to understand audience demographics, popular content, and referral sources. Jetpack Analytics integrates with Google Analytics for more advanced tracking options.

Benefits of Using Built-in Analytics

Easy Accessibility – Website builders' built-in analytics are typically easily accessible from the website's backend or dashboard, eliminating the need for separate tools or complex configurations.

User-Friendly Interface – These tools are designed to be user-friendly, allowing website owners of varying technical abilities to understand and utilize the data effectively.

Relevant Metrics – Website builders often focus on providing essential metrics specific to website performance, such as page views, traffic sources, and visitor behavior. This enables users to gain key data without getting overwhelmed by unnecessary data.

Integration Capabilities – Some website builders allow integration with popular external tools like Google Analytics. This enables users to combine the benefits of both tools and access more advanced tracking and reporting features.

Real-time Data – Built-in tools often provide real-time or near real-time data, allowing website owners to monitor their site's performance as it happens. This enables timely decision-making and optimization.

It's important to note that the specific features and capabilities of each website builder's analytic tool may vary. Therefore, it's recommended to explore the policy documentation or support resources provided by the website builder of your choice to understand the full extent of their analytics offerings.

Free and Paid Tools

When it comes to website analytics, taking advantage of the built-in tools provided by website builders can be a great starting point. These often offer information about your website's performance, visitor behavior, and traffic sources, all without any additional cost. However, it's important to understand that the capabilities of free built-in analytics may have limitations compared to more robust paid solutions.

By utilizing the free options provided by website builders, you will gain a basic understanding of your website's performance, identify popular content, and track essential metrics. This information helps with optimizing content, improving user experience, and refining your marketing plans.

However, as your website grows and your analytical needs become more advanced, investing in paid analytics can offer additional benefits. Paid and free analytics tools, such as SEMrush or other third-party platforms mentioned in the earlier section, often provide more comprehensive features, customizable reports, and advanced tracking selections. They can share a deeper understanding of user behavior, conversion funnels, e-commerce performance, and much more.

If you are considering an investment in your analytical capabilities, enhancing your tools could be highly beneficial. Advanced tools can unlock powerful insights that help you track and measure specific business goals with greater precision. They often include detailed information breakdown, A/B testing, and heatmaps, enabling you to analyze and optimize your website more effectively.

It's important to assess your specific needs, budget, and long-term goals before investing in paid analytics. Evaluate the features and capabilities of different software tools out there and consider whether the additional insights and functionalities they offer align with your objectives.

While free built-in tools are a great starting point, investing in paid ones can provide more advanced features and in-depth analysis. I recommend striking a balance between leveraging the free tools available and considering the potential benefits of paid solutions based on your website's growth and specific requirements.

Free Content Marketing & SEO Tools

Google Rank Checker – A Google Rank Checker allows you to check the ranking of your website or specific pages in Google's search results for certain keywords. The tool can help you track your search engine optimization (SEO) efforts and see how well your website is performing in Google's search results. It can also provide you with insights into your competition and help you identify opportunities for improvement. Some popular examples of Google Rank Checker Tools include Ahrefs, Moz, SEMrush, and SERPstat.

Headline Generator Tool – A Headline Generator generates headlines for content such as articles, blog posts, and advertisements. The tool uses algorithms and/or natural language processing to suggest headlines based on keywords, topics, or other input. The goal of a Headline Generator Tool is to help users create attention-grabbing and informative headlines that will entice readers to click and read further. These tools can be useful for content creators, marketers, and advertisers who want to improve the visibility and engagement of their content online. Examples of Headline Generator Tools include CoSchedule Headline Analyzer, Portent's Content Idea Generator, and HubSpot's Blog Topic Generator.

Keyword Density Tool – A Keyword Density Tool analyzes a piece of text, such as a website page or a blog post, to determine the number of times a keyword or phrase appears in relation to the total number of words on the page. The tool calculates the keyword density, which is expressed as a percentage, and provides insights into how well a page is optimized for a specific keyword or phrase. Keyword density is used as an indicator of search engine optimization (SEO) because search engines consider keyword density when ranking pages in search results. A high keyword density is seen as an indicator that the page is over-optimized and may result in a lower ranking, while a low keyword density may indicate that the page is not optimized enough for the target keyword. Examples of Keyword Density Tools include SEO Book Keyword Density Analyzer and WebConfs.com Keyword Density Checker.

Google Keyword Planner Tool – Google Keyword Planner is free, and it is provided by Google AdWords for advertisers to research keywords for their search and display campaigns. It allows users to search for keywords and see data such as estimated monthly searches, competition level, and suggested bids for those keywords. The tool also provides suggestions for related keywords that may be useful for campaigns. The Google Keyword Planner Tool is used for both paid and organic search engine optimization (SEO) efforts, as the data it provides can be valuable for understanding the search volume and competition for specific keywords. In addition to keyword research, the tool can also help with ad campaign planning and budgeting by providing estimated costs for advertising on Google.

Keyword Gap Analysis – A Keyword Gap Analysis helps identify the differences in keyword usage and ranking between two or more websites. The tool compares the keywords used by competing websites to determine which keywords they have in common, which keywords they rank for, and which keywords they are not ranking for. This information can be used to identify opportunities for improvement in search engine optimization (SEO) and to help create a more effective keyword strategy. Keyword Gap Analysis Tools can be especially useful for businesses and websites that are looking to compete with other websites in the same industry or niche. Examples of Keyword Gap Analysis Tools include SEMrush, Ahrefs, and Moz.

Page Speed Analysis – A Page Speed Analysis measures the time it takes for a website page to load and provides recommendations for optimizing the page's performance. These tools test the website's page speed, which is an important factor for both user experience and search engine optimization (SEO). Faster page speed can result in improved user engagement and better search engine rankings. Page Speed Analysis Tools often provide detailed information on the time it takes for different elements of the page to load, such as images, scripts, and stylesheets. They also provide recommendations for reducing page load times, such as optimizing images, minifying code, and using a fast-hosting provider. Examples of Page Speed Analysis Tools include GTmetrix, Google PageSpeed Insights, and Pingdom Website Speed Test.

Content Readability Tool – A Content Readability Tool assesses the readability of things such as a blog post, article, or web page. It uses algorithms to evaluate various factors such as sentence length, vocabulary complexity, and grammar to determine the reading level of the text. The goal of a Content Readability Tool is to help writers and content creators produce texts that are easy to understand and engaging for their target audience. The results of the readability analysis can be used to improve the text by making it more accessible and readable for a wider audience. Examples of Content Readability Tools include the Flesch-Kincaid Reading Ease Score, the Gunning Fog Index, and the SMOG Index.

Word Counter Tool – A Word Counter counts the number of words in a piece of text, such as a blog post, article, or essay. The tool is often used by writers and content creators to determine the length of their text, track their writing progress, and ensure that their text meets specific word count requirements. Some Word Counter Tools also provide additional information such as character count, reading time, and speaking time, which can be useful for optimizing the text for different purposes, such as online publishing or speech delivery. Examples of Word Counter Tools include WordCounter.net, Writing Metrics, and the word counter in Google Docs and Microsoft Word.

Optimizing E-Commerce Metrics

Most of what I've shared is about checking resources that give you useful information. Now, armed with this info, your next step is to look for specific things that help you figure out what actions to take based on what you see.

Tracking key performance indicators (KPIs) is super useful for this—it helps you measure how well you are doing online and make smart conclusions. In the next part, I'll tell you about important signs to see if your online store is doing well or needs improvements. I'll also give you tips on what to do with the info, along with a few examples to help you understand better.

Conversion Rate

The conversion rate is a pivotal metric, revealing the percentage of website visitors who engage in a desired action, such as completing a purchase. For instance, if 100 visitors come to your online store and 10 of them make a purchase, your conversion rate is 10%.

It's essential to note that on an e-commerce website, a conversion isn't solely limited to making a purchase; it can also include actions like signing up for a newsletter, creating an account, or downloading a resource.

Determining whether your conversion rate is good or bad depends on various factors, including the industry type. As a general guideline, a good conversion rate for e-commerce typically ranges from 2% to 5%, while other industries might have different benchmarks. For instance, sectors like B2B services might consider a 5% conversion rate as impressive, whereas a content-based website might aim for a higher rate due to its distinct goals.

A robust conversion rate indicates that your website effectively persuades visitors to take desired actions based on industry standards. Regularly monitoring and analyzing your conversion rate using tools like Google Analytics allows you to pinpoint potential challenges and devise industry-specific strategies for enhancement.

This ongoing evaluation enables you to adapt and optimize various elements, content, and user experiences on your website for a more effective and industry-relevant conversion process.

Average Order Value (AOV)

Average Order Value (AOV) represents the average monetary value of transactions conducted on your platform. It serves as a barometer for understanding customer spending behavior that influences your overall revenue. When the AOV experiences an upward trend, it indicates that customers are either buying more items or opting for higher-priced products during each transaction, thereby contributing to a boost to your financial performance.

To enhance your AOV, consider implementing effective sales tactics. One approach is to encourage upselling, where customers are persuaded to purchase a more premium or upgraded version of a product they are interested in. Cross-selling, suggesting complementary items that go together with the customer's selected product, is another avenue to explore. Additionally, offering bundled deals or packages can entice customers to spend more by providing perceived value and convenience.

In essence, by delving into the intricacies of AOV and employing targeted strategies like upselling and cross-selling. This helps to gauge and understand customer spending patterns and proactively work toward maximizing the revenue potential of each transaction on your e-commerce platform.

Customer Acquisition Cost (CAC)

Understanding the cost of acquiring a new customer helps determine the efficiency of your marketing strategies. If your CAC is higher than the revenue generated from a customer, it may indicate an unsustainable business model. Strive to balance your CAC with customer lifetime value (CLV) to ensure long-term profitability. Customer lifetime value is the predicted net profit a customer will generate throughout their entire relationship with a business. Google Analytics tool also shows you your CLV.

Cart Abandonment Rate

Cart abandonment occurs when visitors add items to their shopping carts but leave the website without completing the purchase. A high abandonment rate may indicate issues with the checkout process, unexpected costs, or a lack of trust. Regularly review and optimize your checkout process to minimize cart abandonment and improve overall conversion rates.

Customer Retention Rate

Repeating customers is valuable for the long-term success of your e-commerce business. A high customer retention rate indicates that your products, services, and customer experience are meeting or exceeding expectations. Implement loyalty programs, personalized marketing campaigns, and excellent customer service to foster customer loyalty and increase retention.

Website Traffic and Source Analysis

Monitoring website traffic provides information on the effectiveness of your marketing channels. Analyze the sources of your traffic, such as directly from pop-up venues, organic search, social media, and paid advertising, to identify which channels are driving the most engaged visitors. Allocate resources to the most effective channels to maximize your ROI.

Mobile Responsiveness and User Experience

With the increasing use of mobile devices, a mobile-responsive website is required. Evaluate your website's performance on various devices and ensure a seamless user experience. Slow-loading pages, complicated navigation, or a non-intuitive design can drive potential customers away.

Feedback and Reviews

Customer feedback and reviews offer information on the strengths and weaknesses of your e-commerce website. Positive reviews can build trust and attract new customers, while negative feedback highlights areas for improvement. Actively collect and respond to customer reviews to demonstrate your commitment to customer satisfaction.

Regularly monitoring these key indicators is essential for maintaining a successful e-commerce website. Understanding and acting upon these metrics helps with optimizing your online store, improving customer satisfaction, and driving long-term growth.

Remember that continuous adaptation and improvement are necessary for staying ahead in the competitive online marketplace.

TRACK AND ANALYZE WORKSHEET – Measure Performance.

1. How is data compared to special magnifying glasses in the narrative, and what does it help you to see more clearly?

_____

_____

_____

_____

2. What information can search engine tools provide about your website's performance?

_____

_____

_____

_____

3. Briefly explain the purpose of Google Analytics, Google Search Console, and Google Business Profile.

_____

_____

_____

_____

4. How does Google Business Profile benefit local businesses, especially those running pop-up shops?

_____

_____

_____

_____

SECRET GUIDE #10
Stay Committed to the Grind

Persistently Thrive & Celebrate Small Wins.

Enduring Online Popupreneurship

T hankfully, as entrepreneurs in the 21st century, we have the luxury of operating accessible online storefronts, using e-commerce and digital marketing to build and grow our businesses. However, amidst the development of online business, there is a time-tested strategy that has withstood the test of time that you've read about, become actionable, and will serve you as the e-commerce growth engine secret: "*The Pop-up Shop Business.*"

Much of my inspiration for enduring online popupreneurship comes from two of my greatest life mentors. This section is a tribute to the remarkable stories of my grandmothers, Beryl and Euphema, who collectively dedicated a hundred years to the art of pop-up shop operations. By probing into their experiences, we can unearth lessons that reverberate with modern-day entrepreneurs seeking success online.

Picture this: a bygone era in Jamaica, WI, where technology and digital marketing were virtually nonexistent. Yet, despite these limitations, my grandmothers thrived in their pop-up shop business endeavors without the aid of e-commerce shops or social media posts. Their success hinged on their work ethic and an unyielding commitment to their craft. Today, we have the advantage of numerous online tools and resources that simplify the pop-up shop experience, including this very publication. Therefore, it is best to acknowledge the level of "grinding" and dedication required by entrepreneurs in the present era pales in comparison to the arduous challenges faced by our predecessors.

When we speak of "grinding" in this secret, I refer to the strategic efforts undertaken to achieve goals amidst the myriad obstacles that present themselves along the entrepreneurial journey. It is about extracting the best from the worst situations and developing an astute ability to navigate through the uncharted territories of business.

With that, I coined the term "wizapreneur," of whom was my grandmother's. Wizapreneur encapsulates the spirit of entrepreneurs who possess wisdom and embrace the simpler things in life and business. As you strive to accomplish this, a few operational aspects will emerge that will require little patience and fortitude.

One of the key parts of pop-up shop operations lies in the art of selecting appropriate venues during the offseason. While the digital online space offers immense possibilities, there is a distinct value in appreciating the outdoors and engaging with customers face-to-face. It is a refreshing departure from the screen-centric world that often dominates our lives as online business owners. By embracing the world beyond computer screens and smartphones, we establish a genuine connection with our target audience that extends far beyond mere transactions.

Staying committed to your online and offline business is a badge of honor, especially during those challenging times when revenues may be down and the dry spell season is upon us. It is during these moments that the true spirit of entrepreneurship shines through. Remember the resilience of my grandmothers, the first two wizapreneurs, and draw inspiration from their dedication. They endured slow seasons, economic downturns, and limited resources, yet they pressed on with determination. Their stories described in Secret Guide #9 in "*Popup Your Startup*" serve as a testament to the enduring power of passion, perseverance, and an unyielding commitment to one's purpose.

As you continue your journey, let the lessons from these pop-up shop pioneers be of encouragement. Embrace the technology at your disposal, but also cherish the simplicity and authenticity that face-to-face interactions bring. Seek out appropriate venues to establish your pop-up shops, recognizing the untapped potential of offline engagement. Above all, remain steadfast in your commitment to your business, even when the odds seem stacked against you. Remember, the pop-up shop is not merely a business operation; it is proof of the untiring human spirit that drives you to create, innovate, elevate, and succeed.

So, if you are one of the wizapreneurs out there, may you forge ahead with wisdom, courage, and a deep appreciation for the timeless art of pop-up shops. Together, let us build a future where technology and tradition harmoniously coexist, empowering entrepreneurs to carve their own paths and create lasting legacies.

Secrets of Pop-up Shop Success

As an online entrepreneur or small business owner, please understand that growth comes in various forms, often requiring you to step out of your comfort zone and undertake less glamorous or popular territories. Popping up your e-commerce business through pop-up shop processes is one such endeavor that tests your mettle and reveals how far you're willing to go to achieve tremendous success. In this discussion, we will examine deeper into the secret scenarios and instances you may face as a popupreneur. This is specifically tailored to those of you who are determined to win at all costs.

Becoming an Overachieving Popupreneur

Thriving and celebrating small wins, even in the face of challenging times or moments of doubt, is what sets winners apart from the rest. It is during these moments that your commitment to the grind truly shines through, earning you the coveted badge of an overachieving popupreneur. This distinction is not to be taken lightly, as it signifies a level of dedication, resilience, and resourcefulness. Let us strive together to become overachieving popupreneurs.

Unconventional Growth — The first secret to success lies in recognizing that growth comes in many forms, and not all of them are glamorous or popular. Claiming the power of pop-up shops requires you to step outside online and engage with customers in a more tangible way. It will involve setting up temporary physical locations, attending events and fairs, or partnering with local businesses for collaborative pop-up experiences. Embracing these opportunities allows you to tap into new markets, reach a wider audience, and create memorable moments. Remember, the path to success is not always in a straight line or conventional, but by being open to unconventional avenues, you position yourself for exponential growth.

Mindset Mastery — Another secret lies in the mindset mastery of an overachieving popupreneur (OP). *Mindset Mastery* is the proactive cultivation of a growth-oriented mentality, emphasizing resilience, celebration of small achievements, and self-reward, which is crucial for navigating challenges and achieving long-term success as an entrepreneur. You will undoubtedly face setbacks and moments of distrust. It is in these moments that your true character and determination are tested. Instead of succumbing to negativity or giving up, embrace a growth mindset and find opportunities for learning and improvement. Celebrate every milestone, no matter how small, as they are steppingstones toward your ultimate success. It's the daily grind and consistency that ultimately leads to long-term triumph. Also, treat yourself following small victories. Take a day off and go to the movies with friends, or take a few hours off to read a book you have always wanted to start reading. Visit the spa. A little self-care doesn't hurt. Buy yourself a new outfit. Because you deserve it. The point is to reward yourself for a job well done, no matter how small. Doing this will make everything worth the effort. And don't forget to reward and acknowledge your team efforts as well.

Pinnacle Popupreneur – Furthermore, the badge of an OP is not just about business success; it encompasses the values of commitment and perseverance. It shows your ability to weather storms and stay true to your vision, even when faced with adversity. It's about going the extra mile for your customers, providing exceptional service, and building a reputation that speaks volumes about your dedication. When you embody the qualities of an OP, you create a ripple effect that extends beyond your business, inspiring others, including your team, to strive for greatness.

To become an OP, it is crucial to continually seek growth and push the boundaries of your comfort zone. Seek openings for collaboration, innovation, and experimentation. Stay attuned to market trends, customer preferences, and technological advancements that can enhance your pop-up shop initiative. Be open to feedback, both from your customers and peers, as it provides direction for improvement.

Becoming an overachieving popupreneur requires a combination of passion, and a growth mindset. It's about seizing breaks, thriving, and celebrating small wins along the way. By adopting these secrets and embodying the spirit of an OP, you position yourself to the pinnacle of success. So, let's continue or pursue this journey together, armed with the wisdom of the past and enthusiasm for the future, as we redefine the boundaries of pop-ups and pave the way for our own extraordinary legacies and professional apex.

Grinder's Triumph – We are still marching toward becoming an OP. Acknowledge that achieving specific business goals and winning in the competitive marketplace requires dedication and a willingness to confront the challenges that come with popping up your e-commerce business. While it may not be a glamorous endeavor, the framework of "*Popup Your E-commerce*" holds immense potential for success. Your effort will demand your grinding, so stay committed.

If we examine the statistics on the failures of small e-commerce businesses, it becomes evident that the road to substantial success is far from easy. You may face numerous hurdles in navigating the highly competitive marketplace, regardless of your industry. This is precisely why finding your blue ocean, as discussed in Secret Guide #2, holds such significance. Imagine having already established and operated an online business, investing time and effort into SEO and marketing, and then suddenly pivoting to operate offline pop-up shops or brick-and-mortar establishments. If you find yourself in that position, you are undoubtedly a true grinder, as per my definition. Keep pushing forward, for you have reached the last but certainly not the least important guide of this book, which further underscores the importance of your commitment to the grind and triumph.

Success Mastery – Now, allow me to shed light on a lesson that holds significant weight—no event your business participates in can be deemed a failure. You may find it intriguing or even bewildering, but it holds a key secret to success mastery. *Success mastery* in pop-up shop business is transforming challenges into wins through adaptability, creativity, and innovation, prioritizing the quality of interactions, infusing unique brand personality, and maintaining a flexible, open-minded approach to achieve resounding success in every scenario. Take a moment to breathe then reflect on the following sentence: "Essentially, no event that your business participates in can be a failure." Read it twice if necessary. This concept sums up an understanding that will transform your perspective on pop-up shops, regardless of their scale, location, or timing.

Please join me for this enlightening perspective. Imagine yourself participating in a grand affair or a low-traffic farmers market situated in the middle of nowhere, perhaps even in the freezing cold winter months. From a conventional standpoint, these scenarios might be viewed as less desirable or even potentially unsuccessful ventures. However, as an OP, you possess the ability to turn any event into a resounding success. How? By exercising the power of adaptation, creativity, and innovation.

For instance, at a grand affair, you can make a memorable impact by crafting a pop-up experience that leaves attendees in awe. By incorporating interactive elements, exclusive promotions, or unique collaborations, you can create a buzz around your brand and leave a lasting impression on potential customers. On the other hand, when participating in a low-traffic farmers market or amid winter, you can tap into the power of intimacy. Engage with each visitor on a deeper level, offer tailored recommendations, and cultivate a sense of warmth and hospitality that sets your business apart.

The key to succeeding at any pop-up event lies in your ability to adapt and tailor your approach to specific circumstances. It is not solely about the quantity of attendees but the quality of interactions and the lasting impact you create. By infusing your pop-up shop with your brand's unique personality and providing an exceptional customer experience, you ensure that every event becomes a springboard toward achieving your business goals.

As an OP, remain flexible and open-minded, commit to the grind, and continuously strive for excellence and success mastery. Embrace the unexpected, view challenges as opportunities, and innovate within the constraints of each event. Remember, the journey to success is not linear, and every pop-up event presents a chance for growth and learning.

Recognize that no event is inherently a failure with success mastery in mind. By reframing our perspective, embracing adaptability, and infusing each pop-up event with your brand's unique essence, you can transform any occasion into a resounding success. So, progress onward, armed with the lessons of the past and the knowledge that every pop-up experience holds the potential to catapult your business to new heights.

Resilient Pathways to Success

When it comes to pop-up shops and their adaptation to e-commerce, they are more robust and less prone to failure than traditional methods. Let's break down why these "pop-ups" are considered resilient pathways to success.

Low-Cost and Low-Risk Nature – Pop-up businesses stand out because they require much less upfront investment compared to traditional ventures like brick-and-mortar stores. Traditional businesses involve hefty expenses for things like renting a space, buying equipment, and hiring staff. In contrast, pop-up events have a significantly lower financial commitment. This allows you to test your ideas, especially when starting a new online business. This provides less risk, refining strategies, and understanding your audience without a huge financial burden. *Example: Hosting a pop-up event in a local park or using a temporary space instead of a permanent storefront.*

Unique and Unconventional Venues – Pop-up events often happen in unusual locations, adding to their appeal. Holding a concert in an abandoned warehouse or setting up a pop-up restaurant in a park creates a memorable experience that stands out. This uniqueness attracts more attendees and sets pop-ups apart from traditional venues. *Example: Choosing a distinctive venue for a fashion pop-up event, like an art gallery or an old warehouse.*

Experiential and Interactive Nature – They are not just about showcasing products; they involve attendees as active participants. This interaction builds a stronger connection between the audience and the brand online and offline, increasing the chances of repeat attendance, social media buzz, and word-of-mouth. Engaging activities and immersive experiences leave a lasting impression. *Example: Setting up interactive displays or organizing workshops during a pop-up market.*

Flexibility and Agility – Pop-ups can quickly adapt to changes in consumer demand, emerging trends, or seasonal variations. Unlike permanent establishments, your temporary shop can pivot or relocate fast, maximizing reach and capitalizing on opportunities. This adaptability keeps your company relevant to the dynamic needs and preferences of the audience. *Example: Adjusting product offerings online based on customer feedback during a pop-up event.*

While these shops offer advantages that make them less likely to fail, success still requires careful planning, precise execution, and effective management. Challenges such as limited capacity or shorter timelines need strategic thinking. These challenges are addressed in *"Popup Your Startup."* In addition, understanding and effectively expressing your company's value provides a solid foundation for a high-performance and path to success.

Pop-ups shouldn't be underestimated in their resilience and success path. Their low-cost nature, unique venues, experiential qualities, and adaptability make them strong platforms for you to showcase your offerings by initiating an **omnichannel** connection with the audience, which drives your businesses forward. With these advantages and planning thoughtfully, unlock new levels of growth and prosperity.

Unveiling Your Value Proposition

Make sure to clearly explain what makes your company special. Understand who you're talking to and what they really want. Match your product or service with what they need to create a strong and attractive offer. If you want more info on this, revisit Secret Guide #3 of this book.

Articulate your value proposition to craft a focused and precise message during your sales presentation at various venues. Clearly show how your product or service directly addresses the challenges faced by your target audience and offer a viable solution. Highlight the unique features, benefits, and attributes (FAB), illustrating why your offering is the best choice.

With novelty, adopting creative and engaging methods such as demonstrations, interactive displays, or experiential marketing brings your product or service to life. Captivate the customer's attention so they fully grasp the value that your company brings.

In essence, knowing and unveiling a unique value proposition, identifying the right target audience, delivering a well-focused purpose, and employing novelty to showcase your offering are components of building a thriving e-commerce storefront that operates pop-up shops. Doing this further attract and direct the attention of potential customers to your e-commerce website.

Creating a robust value proposition requires persistent effort. As your business progresses, which is inevitable, your value proposition should evolve accordingly. Consistently refine and communicate it as needed to keep your business pertinent, engaging, and appealing.

For instance, imagine you run a tech company offering software solutions. Continuously gathering user feedback, staying updated on emerging tech trends, and adapting your value proposition to highlight innovative features can help maintain your competitive edge. As the tech landscape evolves, so should your value proposition to showcase the latest advancements and ensure your solution aligns with the current needs of your target market.

Presentation and Tracking Event Benchmarks

In declaring an OP status, it becomes evident that following through on the earlier insights is key to unlocking your true potential. Among these steps lies the art of crafting a flawless presentation, taking shoppers on a journey that captivates their attention and leaves a lasting impression.

Additionally, understanding the benchmarks established for each event and utilizing them as metrics for success is vital. These benchmarks involve various aspects, including revenue goals, email list signups, scans of QR codes or captured URLs, and data on high-ticket merchandise. To successfully track these benchmarks, I have developed what I call a "directive"—a written guide that has yielded great results for my own pop-up operations. My team, too, has embraced this directive, utilizing it to streamline their performance measurement. This ensures that expectations are met and keeps everyone focused on achieving the desired results. The directive I have created outlines the monetary targets that must be achieved and the number of email signups required for each event. Allow me to share with you some recommended items that you can incorporate into your own directive sheet.

The success of your company extends beyond immediate sales at events. While executing flawlessly at your booth is essential, one of your primary objectives is to cultivate long-lasting e-commerce customers. Building upon the guidance provided in Secret Guide #2, you can create an environment at your pop-ups that encourages guests to engage with your business online. This brings us to yet another secret: developing a website that not only entertains but also engages and educates your visitors. It is important to recognize that if your events may not always yield immediate results at the grassroots level, you can still create a thriving online presence through your website. By showcasing the value your business offers and nurturing relationships with potential customers, you lay the foundation for future conversions and sales. Patience is key throughout this process, as the true impact of your efforts may not manifest immediately. However, with firm belief in yourself and your team, coupled with consistent work, you will witness the fruition of your endeavors.

Furthermore, as you continue to refine your operations, it is essential to understand the systems you have developed and ensure they are easily replicable for others to follow. By establishing a well-defined and documented process, you can streamline your operations, empower your team, and ensure consistency across your pop-up events. This framework serves as a blueprint for success, guiding your team and facilitating seamless execution.

Nailing your presentation and tracking event benchmarks are components of becoming an OP. By inviting your audience with a well-crafted presentation, you foster a deeply absorbing ambience. Simultaneously, by utilizing benchmarks and implementing a directive, you can effectively measure and track your progress, ensuring that you are on the path to success. Remember, success may not always be immediate, but by believing in the process, being patient, and building a robust online presence, you pave the way for long-term growth. Embrace the secrets and guidance provided and unleash your potential as an unstoppable force in the world of pop-ups and e-commerce.

Navigating Unexpected Events with Ease

In the pursuit of success, mastering the art of presentation and effectively tracking event benchmarks are components of the pop-up shop framework. Additionally, it is important to recognize the significance of having a business contingency plan. While focusing on presentations and achieving measurable goals is crucial, preparing for unexpected events is what makes entrepreneurs great. Unforeseen circumstances such as market shifts, economic downturns, or natural disasters can disrupt even the most well-executed plans. Therefore, understanding the importance of a business contingency plan and its role in navigating unexpected events with ease becomes paramount. Here I will briefly share the significance of having a robust contingency plan and explore actionable strategies that you can implement to safeguard your pop-ups and ensure continuity in the face of adversity. By combining the power of nailing presentations and tracking event benchmarks with the foresight of a well-prepared contingency plan, you can unleash your true grinding potential and successfully navigate the unpredictable terrain.

Be well-prepared to tackle unforeseen circumstances that may disrupt operation. The implementation of a contingency plan serves as a fundamental tool in mitigating potential risks and minimizing the impact of unexpected events. Up next, explore the importance of a contingency plan in various business scenarios, highlighting its role in minimizing downtime, protecting revenue, maintaining customer trust, ensuring business continuity, and mitigating risks.

Minimizing Downtime – One of the key advantages of having a contingency plan in place is the ability to minimize downtime during critical situations. Whether it be sudden cancellations, unexpected mishaps such as a broken vehicle or damaged merchandise, or adverse weather conditions, businesses equipped with contingency strategies can swiftly pivot their operations. By promptly adapting to these challenges, you can significantly reduce the duration and extent of disruptions, enabling you to resume normal operations without prolonged delays.

Protecting Revenue – A well-structured contingency plan serves as a shield for businesses, safeguarding their revenue streams amidst unforeseen events. In instances where salespeople fail to show up or other unexpected staffing issues arise, a contingency plan provides alternative strategies to ensure revenue generation. By diversifying sales channels, employing backup plans, or leveraging technological solutions, you can safeguard your financial stability and mitigate potential losses.

Maintaining Customer Trust – Customer trust is an asset for any business, and a contingency plan plays a crucial role in preserving it during challenging times. When unexpected events occur, customers rely on businesses to promptly address their needs and concerns. By having a backup plan, organizations demonstrate their commitment to customer satisfaction, reinforcing trust and loyalty. Swift and effective responses, alternative service options, and transparent communication help maintain strong customer relationships, even in the face of challenges.

Ensuring Business Continuity – Business continuity is vital for the long-term success of any organization. A well-crafted contingency plan enables businesses to navigate through crises and disruptions, ensuring that essential operations remain functional. By identifying critical business functions and developing strategies to address potential risks, companies can effectively continue their operations, minimizing the impact of unexpected events. This proactivity builds resilience and enhances an organization's ability to withstand adversity.

Mitigating Risk – Risk mitigation is a part of effective business management, and a contingency plan serves as a comprehensive risk management tool. By conducting thorough risk assessments and developing strategies, organizations can identify potential vulnerabilities and create preventive measures. Proactive risk mitigation measures not only reduce the likelihood of disruptions but also minimize the severity of their consequences. Through continuous evaluation and refinement of the contingency plan, businesses adapt to evolving risks and emerging challenges, bolstering their overall resilience.

The importance of a well-designed contingency plan cannot be overstated. By preparing for the unexpected, businesses can minimize downtime, protect revenue, maintain customer trust, ensure business continuity, and mitigate risks effectively. As the global market becomes increasingly unpredictable, organizations that invest in developing and implementing contingency plans position themselves for success, proving their ability to navigate through adversity and emerge stronger than before. Revisit the Secret Guide #7 of "*Popup Your Startup*" on how to do a contingency plan.

Whichever of these you stumble upon, you will be guaranteed a winner. These guidelines will not work just by mundanely doing them. They must be done with a strong belief and optimism. My pop-up bulletproof-to-failure list here will work every time if you believe and continuously practice them.

Pop-up Success Boost

Operating an e-commerce business has its own set of advantages, allowing entrepreneurs to tap into the vast potential of the online market. However, by using offline pop-up shops in its strategy, you can unlock even greater opportunities to excel. In this discussion, I will go over various ways to leverage pop-ups to deliver enormous results during the busy seasons.

Capitalize on Revenue Growth – Capitalizing on revenue growth is a primary goal for any entrepreneur. Pop-up shops provide a unique avenue to achieve this objective by establishing temporary physical retail spaces, which tap into the immediate shopping needs and impulses of customers. Pop-up shops attract a diverse range of shoppers who may not have been aware of or considered shopping online. The face-to-face interaction and tactile experience offered by pop-up shops can often lead to impulse purchases, thereby increasing sales and revenue.

Connect with Shoppers – Connecting with pop-up shoppers and directing them to shop online is a strategy for e-commerce entrepreneurs to follow. While pop-up shops provide an offline shopping experience, it is essential to capitalize on this opportunity to convert these customers into online shoppers. To achieve this, entrepreneurs like yourself can use various tactics. For example, they can provide incentives for customers to sign up for their online store's newsletter or offer exclusive discounts on online purchases. By nurturing the relationship with pop-up shop customers and including them in the online shopping experience, entrepreneurs expand their customer base and grow revenue.

Increase Event Frequency – Another key aspect of successful pop-up shop operations is the frequency of events. To deliver enormous results, you should aim to participate in as many pop-up events as possible, particularly during the peak seasons. This not only increases brand exposure but also allows tapping into the large pool of potential pop-up shop attendees. Selecting events based on target audience demographics and preferences helps maximize reach and generate higher sales volumes.

Delegate Sales Members – Delegating the sales team to manage pop-up events is prudent and ensures smooth operations and maximize productivity. It's best to assign experienced sales personnel to handle the pop-up shops, enabling effective customer engagement, providing product information, and facilitating sales. Having a dedicated team at venues frees up time for you to focus on other parts of the business while ensuring that customers receive personalized attention and a positive shopping experience.

Product Testing Opportunity – Pop-up shops also provide the testing of e-commerce products in a real-world retail environment. Use this to gauge your customer preferences, gather feedback, and identify any necessary improvements or modifications. This also can be applied to optimize the online shopping experience and enhance product offerings. Conducting such tests during pop-up events assists in refining online strategy, tailoring product offerings, and delivering more appealing and relevant online shopping.

Incorporating offline pop-up shop operations into an e-commerce business strategy can deliver enormous results during the busy pop-up shop seasons. While capitalizing on revenue growth, please connect with pop-up shoppers and drive them to shop online as well. Participating in numerous events, delegating to the sales team, and testing online products aids in customer base expansion, increases sales, and enhances overall performance.

Lean Months Success Strategies

Operating a business comes with its own set of challenges, and one of the most significant hurdles is navigating through the lean months when sales are slower. However, with the right plans and proactive approaches, entrepreneurs can turn these lean periods into opportunities for growth and success. Here, we will explore several effective techniques that can help you maximize your efforts during the lean months, such as seeking indoor venues, improving online performance, following up with loyal fans, refining systems and processes, and scouting for prospective positions to fill. Additionally, I will discuss the importance of rationing reserved funds or capital to keep your business afloat during these slower seasons.

Seeking Indoor Venues and Participating in Winter Markets – When the winter months roll around, it's essential to adapt your business strategy to the changing climate. I suggest you seek indoor venues for your operations. By booking indoor pop-ups during this time, you provide your customers with comfortable shopping, shielded from the harsh weather conditions. Indoor venues offer a warm and inviting atmosphere, attracting more prospects who may otherwise prefer to stay indoors.

Furthermore, participating in winter markets showcases your products and engages with a wider audience. Winter markets often attract a diverse range of shoppers looking for unique and seasonal items. By setting up a booth or stall in these markets, you can tap into the existing foot traffic and introduce your brand to new customers who may not have come across your online store.

Doubling Down on Online Growth – While offline execution is crucial during the lean months, it's equally important to double down on online growth efforts. With more people spending time indoors and browsing the internet, the online marketplace becomes even more competitive. Therefore, focusing on enhancing your website performance is vital for sustained success.

As I have shared numerous times, a way to improve a site is by investing in targeted digital marketing campaigns. During the lean times, continue to utilize social media platforms, search engine optimization techniques, and paid advertising to increase your brand visibility and reach a broader audience. Take advantage of the slower pop-up shop months to optimize your website, streamline the user experience, and enhance your online store's functionality. Additionally, consider offering special promotions and discounts exclusively for online shoppers during these times, enticing them to make purchases.

Follow Up with Your Loyal Customers – Your loyal customers are the lifeblood of your business. During the lean season, maintain a strong connection with them and remind them of the value your brand offers to their lives. Implement a personalized follow-up strategy, such as sending targeted emails, offering exclusive discounts, or providing sneak peeks of upcoming products or collections to be rolled out at the start of the busy pop-up shop season. By nurturing these relationships, you encourage repeat purchases and continued loyalty.

Refine Your Systems and Processes – The slower months also provide a break for self-reflection and improvement. Take the time to evaluate your systems and processes, identifying any loopholes or areas for enhancement. Review your inventory management, shipping processes, customer support systems, and overall business operations. By addressing inefficiencies and making necessary adjustments, you can streamline your business and provide a better experience for both your team and your customers.

Remember to involve your salesforce in this process as well. Seek their feedback and insights regarding areas that can be improved. Encourage a culture of continuous improvement within your organization, where everyone is committed to making the business holistically better.

Team Growth and Skills Enhancement – During times when operation is a bit slower, spend some time looking for new people to add to your team, especially if you know a busy time is coming soon. This could mean finding new salespeople, office workers, or managers for the warehouse. Finding the right people now will help a lot when things get busier. Look for people who fit well with your company's values, have the right skills, and can help your business grow.

At the same time, you will also use my cross-training methods explained in Secret Guide #8 and train your sales team more skills, like handling online orders. This will make them more flexible and ready to do different jobs when things get busy. Teaching your team more things helps them switch between offline and online tasks easily. This makes things work better and keeps customers happy.

Set Aside Rain Day Funds – To handle months with less cash coming in, it's important to plan your finances well. When times are tough, having a financial safety net is crucial. To build this safety net, save a part of your earnings during the busier months. This fund, often called a "rainy-day" fund, is especially helpful if your online store isn't doing as well as you'd like alongside your pop-up shop. With this fund, you can cover costs like rent, utilities, employee wages, and outsourced services during slower times. By managing this saved money wisely, you can stay stable and manage the ups and downs that come with changing seasons.

Don't let the slower months discourage you from staying committed to the grind. Use these techniques to make the most of these times and achieve growth. Connect with customers by joining indoor markets and winter events. Improve your online presence to reach more people and offset any loss from pop-up stores. Stay in touch with loyal customers, refine your processes, and look for new opportunities. Manage your finances wisely. By being proactive and using these strategies, your business can thrive even during tough times. Over time, your e-commerce business will become stronger, and slow months will become less of a concern. If you're in an area with favorable weather, you can host events all year, ensuring a steady stream of venues offline.

Visionary E-commerce Goal Setting

Be a visionary, constantly thinking ahead and having a clear goal of what you want to accomplish. By setting your sights on the future, you can align your current actions and strategies to drive growth and success. Additionally, staying present and identifying any pitfalls or shortcomings in your current operations allows you to refine them when necessary, ensuring your business remains agile and adaptable in a rapidly changing market.

Setting Clear Goals

To become a visionary in the world of e-commerce pop-up businesses, you need a clear and forward-thinking vision for where you want your business to go. But it's not enough to just dream – you also must work hard in the present moment. This means coming up with game-changing ideas to transform the industry and refining and completing ongoing projects.

When I talk about "plans," I mean a wide range of strategies that are important for your personal growth and business success. You should define your goals and dreams for the short term and the long term and create a logical plan to guide your efforts. These goals can include things like increasing sales, reaching more customers, getting more people to visit your website, keeping employees happy, showing up more often at pop-up events, and improving how often people make purchases.

A part of being a visionary is setting goals that are clear, measurable, achievable, relevant, and time-bound—often referred to as SMART goals. This helps you make realistic plans and take action so you can track progress and adjust as needed. It's important to regularly check and update these goals to make sure they still make sense, given the changing market and the way your business is growing.

Dynamic Growth Trends

The focus should be on making your business grow steadily. To understand how well you're doing, it's important to track your performance daily, monthly, quarterly, and yearly. This will help you see how your business is moving forward. Your growth should show in different parts of your business, like how much you're selling, how many people are visiting your website, how you're getting new customers, how many employees are staying and how many are going, where you're setting up temporary shops, and how often you're turning potential customers into actual buyers.

It's ideal for your business to grow steadily at first and then really take off, just like the shape of a hockey stick. To do this, you need to use the smart strategies in this book, keep getting better at what you offer, and be ready to change with what people want. Look at your business numbers, find out where you can do better, and make decisive choices to keep growing.

Adoptability and Refinement

Being a visionary also requires staying present and actively monitoring your business. Identify any pitfalls, shortcomings, or areas that need refinement and take prompt action to address them. This may involve analyzing customer feedback, conducting further market research, studying competitors, and staying informed.

Maintaining a growth mindset and being open to change is necessary. Embrace innovation and technological advancements to stay ahead. Explore new marketing channels, optimize your website and user experience, and leverage data analytics. By continuously refining and improving your operations, you can enhance your competitive edge and position yourself for ongoing success.

Embracing a visionary mindset enables you to navigate the future of "*Popup Your E-commerce*" business with confidence and purpose. By setting clear goals, driving sustainable growth, and remaining adaptable, you can stay ahead of the competition and capitalize on emerging opportunities. Remember to regularly evaluate your progress, reassess your goals, and make refinements.

Pop-up shops in Retail Evolution

Maintaining a positive outlook and facing challenges head-on is required. Amidst these challenges, victory might be closer than you think. An exciting trend with immense potential for businesses is the rise of pop-ups. As online shopping gains traction and traditional stores grapple with changes, pop-up shops are positioned to shape the future of retail.

Evolving Retail – Retail is changing as people's shopping habits shift. Online shopping's convenience is causing traditional stores, malls, and big retail spaces to see changes in consumer behavior. Empty stores and decreased foot traffic are becoming common. Yet, these changes open a unique opportunity for pop-up shops to fill the gap and attract consumers.

Pop-up Shops' Potential – Pop-up shops are temporary retail spaces that can be set up anywhere, from vacant stores to sponsored events. They bring innovation to retail, enabling businesses to meet with customers in more personal ways. Pop-up shops attract a diverse range of shoppers who may not typically shop in traditional stores or online.

Unrecognized Advantage – Pop-up shops often fly under customers' radar. While permanent stores might face skepticism, pop-up shop owners are rarely questioned similarly. This lack of scrutiny works in favor of pop-up shop owners, allowing them to showcase their offerings without judgment.

Personal Experience Drives Growth

Many entrepreneurs, including myself, have firsthand experience with the impact of pop-up shops. Engaging with communities and participating in events led to notable sales increases. Reflecting on these involvements and lessons learned is valuable for future endeavors. Documenting what works and what doesn't, can offer insights for growth.

Tapping into Hidden Potential – The full potential of pop-up shops is often misjudged. They are more than just a casual endeavor. Pop-up shops hold the potential to drive substantial business growth. By comprehending their unique benefits, entrepreneurs can use pop-up shops to elevate their enterprises. Embrace the pop up shop phenomenon, and with a keen understanding of its advantages, entrepreneurs can navigate the evolving retail landscape and unlock new avenues of success.

By now, you should have a comprehensive grasp of the potential that pop-up shops hold, as demonstrated through various examples and real-life success stories I've shared. However, let's redirect our attention toward strategies that can guarantee personal development, ongoing expansion, and achievement. In the journey of any popupreneur, ongoing education and collaborations are essential components.

Continual Learning and Collaboration

It is imperative to never stop seeking knowledge and learning. Acquire a mindset of continuous growth and improvement. Engage in activities for personal development, such as reading self-help books, attending seminars, participating in workshops, and joining relevant industry communities. These endeavors will help you stay updated on the latest trends, gain fresh ideas, and advance the expertise of both you and your team.

Collaboration with like-minded individuals is another key part of business success. Recognize that you cannot do everything alone. Building a community of peers allows you to share experiences, exchange ideas, and collectively overcome challenges. This collaborative spirit furthers innovation and provides a support system that can significantly enhance your journey as a popupreneur.

Seeking Mentorship and Counsel – Mentorship and counsel are important in personal and professional development. Seek mentors who have expertise in the pop-up shop arena or retail industry as a whole. Their guidance can prove invaluable as you navigate the complexities of running a business effectively. A mentor can provide a fresh perspective, offer leadership in decision-making, and help you avoid common pitfalls.

Remember Your E-commerce Roots – While pop-up shops are an exciting avenue for growth, please remember that you are still an e-commerce business at your core. Pop-up shops serve to further build and expand your company. By combining the strengths of both online and offline, you create an all-inclusive shopping experience.

Staying encouraged and recognizing the potential of pop-up shops can unlock new horizons. Embrace the concept, continue to gain knowledge, collaborate with peers, seek mentorship, and leverage its power to drive growth and success in your endeavors. The journey may have challenges, but with the right mindset and commitment to the grind, you can transform these obstacles into steppingstones toward achieving your goals.

STAY COMMITTED WORKSHEET – Celebrate Small Wins.

1. Define the term "wizapreneur" based on the author's perspective.

_____

_____

_____

_____

_____

2. What distinguishes an overachieving popupreneur (OP) from a regular entrepreneur?

_____

_____

_____

_____

_____

3. Explain the concept of "Mindset Mastery" in the context of an overachieving popupreneur.

_____

_____

_____

_____

_____

4. How can celebrating small wins and practicing self-reward enhance an entrepreneur's journey?

_____

_____

_____

_____

_____

5. Explain the importance of unveiling a unique value proposition for a pop-up shop.

_____

_____

_____

_____

_____

PROS AND CONS

Tying it all Together

In today's highly competitive business environment, entrepreneurs are always seeking innovative ways to expand their customer base and boost sales. One popular model is the integration of pop-up shop operations with e-commerce. This involves opening temporary physical stores in high-traffic locations for a limited time, and then redirecting customers to online. Here, this book thoroughly reconnoiters the pros and cons of integrating pop-up shop operations with e-commerce websites.

Pros

Increased brand awareness: Pop-up shops provide a fantastic opportunity to generate buzz and enhance brand visibility. By opening temporary physical stores, businesses can reach new audiences that may not have previously been familiar with their brand. Customers can interact with products, try them on, touch to feel, and get a sense of the brand's personality, leading to increased brand loyalty and customer retention.

299

Personalized customer experience: Pop-up shops offer a unique and personalized experience for customers. Brands can design physical spaces that reflect their values and create memorable interactions. These shops can also be used to test new products, gather feedback, and adjust the product line based on customer insights.

Increased sales: Pop-up shops can serve as powerful sales tools. By creating a sense of urgency with limited time offers, businesses can drive sales and instill a fear of missing out among customers. Exclusive deals and promotions available only in-store can be used to upsell customers and encourage additional purchases.

Flexibility: Pop-up shops are highly flexible, making them an attractive option for businesses of all sizes. Entrepreneurs can choose the duration and location of their pop-up shops based on their budget and target audience. This flexibility allows for experimentation with different locations and store layouts to find the most effective approach for the brand.

Cons

Potential high upfront costs: Pop-up shops may require a significant initial investment but are not necessary. Rent, staff, marketing materials, and inventory expenses can quickly add up if you fail to follow my guidance. If the pop up chop fails to generate sufficient sales, businesses may experience financial losses. However, with my strategies failure is not an option.

Limited time frame: For businesses that rely on consistent foot traffic to generate sales, the limited time frame of pop-up shops can be a disadvantage. If the shop is only open for a few weeks or months, it may not provide enough time to build a loyal customer base or generate significant revenue. That is why you will continue to bring your customers to all events, online for revenue opportunities, whether you are at a venue or not.

Logistics: Setting up and maintaining pop-up shops involves various logistical challenges. Finding suitable locations, securing permits and licenses, hiring staff, and managing inventory can be complex, particularly for small businesses without much experience in physical retail. So, for that reason, I have laid out how to do so by reading "*Popup Your Startup*" and this book.

Inconsistent customer experience: Integrating pop-up shop operations with e-commerce websites can lead to an inconsistent customer experience. Customers who visit the physical shop may have a different experience than those who shop online. This inconsistency can create confusion and frustration, making it challenging to offer a seamless customer experience across all channels. For that reason, please ensure that you align your brand image as discussed in Secret Guide #3 of this book.

In conclusion, integrating pop-up shop operations with e-commerce businesses can be a powerful marketing plan. It can increase brand awareness, drive sales, and provide a personalized customer experience. However, carefully consider the high upfront costs, limited time frame, logistics, and potential inconsistency in customer experience.

Businesses should assess their goals, budget, and target audience before deciding to pursue this approach. With proper planning and execution, can help your business stand out and drive sales. Remember to leverage social media, collaborate with influencers, offer exclusive deals, and use email marketing to effectively promote the pop-up shop to your dream audience.

ACKNOWLEDGMENTS

I am profoundly grateful for the invaluable lessons learned and the unyielding support received during the creation of my previous book, "*Popup Your Startup*." As I embark on this new journey with "*Popup Your E-commerce*," I'm reminded of the significance of those who have contributed to my growth and success.

I want to express my deepest gratitude to my beloved children for their understanding and support. Their encouragement has fueled my determination.

I extend heartfelt appreciation to my extended family and friends, for their invaluable insights and belief in my vision.

To my loyal customers and the Hampton Roads community, thank you for your support, which has propelled me forward.

I'm indebted to those who offered guidance and mentorship, empowering me to navigate entrepreneurship with confidence.

As I explored e-commerce, I'm inspired by fellow entrepreneurs' collective knowledge and shared experiences.

I pledge to pay forward the kindness and support by sharing the lessons learned in "*Popup Your E-commerce.*"

To everyone, especially Maria Williams, one my long-time mentors, who has contributed to my journey, thank you for your words of encouragement, wisdom, acts of kindness, and steadfast support.

I am deeply grateful for the privilege of sharing this journey with each of you.

With heartfelt appreciation,

Damian Powell

ABOUT THE AUTHOR

Damian's leadership transformed his startup into an industry-defining pop-up business enterprise. He knew it was time to give back to the community, so he launched "The Pop-up Shop Business Initiative." He created this program to share a concept he developed, encouraging entrepreneurs to make pop-up shops the growth engine for their businesses.

As a result of his work with emerging business minds, he collected the best insights from his experience and produced a written form to serve more people.

Damian's most valuable insights are in *"Popup Your Startup,"* *"**Popup Your E-commerce**,"* *"Popup Your Side Hustle,"* and *"Popup Your Storefront"* book series. "The Pop-up shop Business Tetralogy for Entrepreneurs."

REVIEW

Love this book? Don't forget to leave a review!
Every review matters, and it matters a lot!
Head over to Amazon or wherever you purchased this book
from to leave an honest review for me.
I thank you endlessly.

URGENT PLEA!

Thank you for reading my book!

I appreciate all your feedback and would love to hear
what you have to say.

I need your input to make the next version of this book
and my future books better.

Please leave me a helpful review on Amazon, letting me
know what you thought of the book.

Thanks so much!

Damian Powell

ENDNOTES

Secret Guide #1

Powell, Damian. "Popup Your Startup." 2021. Secret Guide #7 "Operation Readiness," Page 195, section titled "Develop a Contingency Plan."

Square Brand Contributor. "8 Types of Pop-Up Events That Can Help Grow Your Business." Forbes, Sep 28, 2021, https://www.forbes.com/sites/square/2021/09/28/8-types-of-pop-up-events-that-can-help-grow-your-business/?sh=362ec6a94012.

Ayesa Lubag. "Pop-Up Events." Jan 28, 2022, https://www.glueup.com/blog/pop-up-events.

Secret Guide #2

Roy Furr. "The 16 Human Desires: Use these in your marketing." https://www.breakthroughmarketingsecrets.com/blog/16-human-desires-use-marketing/.

Jennifer Simonson. "E-Commerce Marketing In 2024: The Ultimate Guide." Forbes, Feb 13, 2024, https://www.forbes.com/advisor/business/software/e-commerce-marketing/.

Catherine Cote. "How to Identify Business & Market Opportunities." Apr 05, 2022, https://online.hbs.edu/blog/post/how-to-identify-business-opportunities.

Amanda Bellucco Chatham. "10 Best AI Content Generators of 2024." Dec 8, 2023, https://www.wix.com/blog/ai-content-generators.

Michael Heckert. "Search Engine Optimization. The Basics of SEO & How to Get Started." Wix, Aug 19, 2021, https://wixreads.wixsite.com/wixportal/post/seo-basics.

Kim, W. Chan, and Renée Mauborgne. Blue Ocean Strategy: How to Create Uncontested Market Space and Make the Competition Irrelevant. Harvard Business Review Press, February 2005.

Secret Guide #3

Crystal Garrett. "How To Create Brand Messaging That Resonates." Mar 28, 2022, https://www.salesforce.com/blog/create-brand-messaging-that-resonates/.

Joe Stych. "How to Craft Your Brand Message (with Template)." Aug 26, 2021, https://zapier.com/blog/brand-message-template/.

Quote: "Waiting for people to come to you is not a strategy."
Russell Brunson (Traffic Secrets, 2020), p. 12.

Secret Guide #4

Phil Masiello. "10 Tips To Supercharge and Scale Your E-Commerce Growth." Jun 29, 2023, https://www.crunchgrowth.com/2023/06/29/supercharge-scale-ecommerce-growth/.

Pradeep Vasudev. "Omnichannel Customer Engagement: How to Manage Effectively." May 31, 2023, https://www.sprinklr.com/blog/omnichannel-customer-engagement/.

Powell, Damian. "Popup Your Startup." 2021. Secret Guide #4 "The Launchpad Principles," Page 75, section titled "Make Pop-up the Engine that Fuels your Launchpad(s)."

Indeed Editorial Team. "12 Tips for Improving Your Customer Service Etiquette." Mar 16, 2023, https://www.indeed.com/career-advice/career-development/customer-service-etiquette.

Quote: "Sell On Purpose" by Spencer Johnson, Larry Wilson (The One Minute Salesperson), p. 24.

Secret Guide #5

"How to Build A Sales Process That Lands Deals Every Time." Aug 03, 2021, https://www.salesforce.com/eu/resources/articles/sales-process/.

Cambria Davies. "The Ultimate Guide to Creating a Sales Process." Aug 10, 2022, https://blog.hubspot.com/sales/sales-process/.

Secret Guide #6

Amelia Pahm. "The Ultimate Guide To Customer Reviews." Aug 6, 2023, https://onecommerce.io/blog/customer-reviews/.

Colin Burton. "13 Best Online Coaching Platforms and Tools." Feb 7, 2024, https://www.thinkific.com/blog/best-online-coaching-platforms/.

Secret Guide #7

Daniel Keyes. "Pop-up Shops Are Paying Off for Retailers." Jun 11, 2019, https://www.businessinsider.com/pop-up-shops-are-an-effective-retail-tactic-2019-6.

Christine Aebischer. "The 16 Best Pop-Up Shop Ideas for 2022." Jan 7, 2021, https://www.nerdwallet.com/article/small-business/pop-up-shop-ideas.

"4 Best Pop-Up Shop POS Systems Sell More Items Now." Jun 4, 2021, https://toppossystem.com/pop-up-shop-pos-systems/.

Erica Seppala. "Clover VS Square: Which POS System Is Best for Your Small Business?" Merchant Maverick, Aug 26, 2021, https://www.merchantmaverick.com/clover-vs-square/.

Secret Guide #8

Jennifer Herrity. "Cross-Training Employees: 7 Effective Tips To Get Started." Feb 3, 2023, https://www.indeed.com/career-advice/career-development/cross-training-employees.

Oracle.com. "What is CRM? The Complete CRM Guide." https://www.oracle.com/cx/what-is-crm/.

Secret Guide #9

Jon Simpson. "Tracking Your Marketing Efforts: Why It's Important And How To Start." Forbes, Oct 6, 2017, https://www.forbes.com/sites/forbesagencycouncil/2017/10/06/tracking-your-marketing-efforts-why-its-important-and-how-to-start/?sh=37e298d331e8.

Secret Guide #10

Powell, Damian. "Popup Your Startup." 2021. Secret Guide #9 "My Grannies Pop-up Shop," Page 230, section titled "Legends of Wisdom Entrepreneurs."

Tom Coleman. "Here's How 5 E-Commerce Brands Used Pop-Up Stores To Get Ahead." https://www.thestore-front.com/mag/heres-how-5-e-commerce-brands-used-pop-ups-to-get-ahead/.

Christopher Sirk. "Embracing Resilience: 5 Ways to Turn Adversity into Success." CRM.org, Jan 29, 2024, https://crm.org/articles/embracing-resilience-5-ways-to-turn-adversity-into-success.

Amanda Bellucco Chatham. Aug 4, 2023, https://www.wix.com/blog/pop-up-shop-ideas.

INDEX

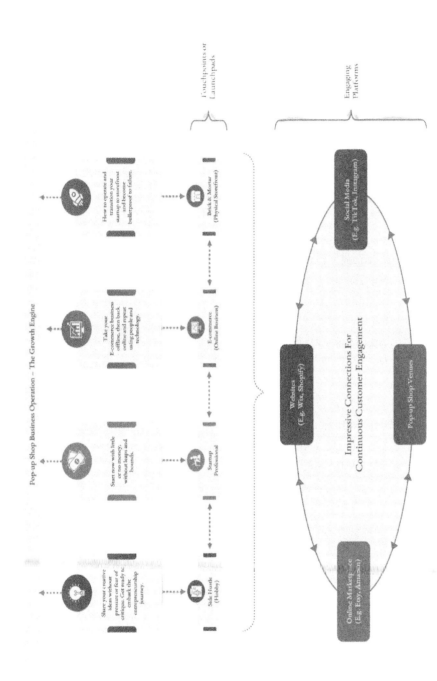

Pop-up Shop Business Operation – The Growth Engine

Share your creative ideas without pressure or fear of critique. Get ready to embark the entrepreneurship journey.

Start now with little or no money; without keeps and bounds.

Take your E-commerce business offline, then back online and repeat using people and technology.

How to operate and transition your startup to storefront and become bulletproof to failure.

Side Hustle (Hobby)

Startup Professional

E-commerce (Online Business)

Brick & Mortar (Physical Storefront)

Touchpoints or Launchpads

Engaging Platforms

Impressive Connections For Continuous Customer Engagement

Social Media (E.g. TikTok, Instagram)

Websites (E.g. Wix, Shopify)

Pop-up Shop Venues

Online Marketplace (E.g. Etsy, Amazon)

Printed in Great Britain
by Amazon

41482396R00192